W9-BDH-735

E-Z REVIEW™

FOR

CRIMINAL LAW

Contributing Editors

Damian S. Jackson, Esq.
Assistant Attorney General
Criminal Prosecution Bureau

Kristine L. Havlik, J.D.
University of Virginia School of Law

Adam C. Rhea, J.D.
University of Virginia School of Law

Consulting Editor
Stephen H. Ruderman, Esq.

Law Review Publishing Corporation
New York, NY 10010
(800) 371-1271

www.lawreviewpublishing.com

Copyright © 2004, 2002, 1999 By

LAW RULES PUBLISHING CORPORATION
1123 Broadway, Suite 509
New York, NY 10010
(800)371-1271

Library of Congress
ISBN 1-887426-80-9

Note: This review publication is not meant to replace required texts as a substitute or otherwise. This publication should not be quoted from or cited to. It is meant only to be used as a reminder of some subject matter and is not a substitute for a comprehensive understanding of the material that it references or outlines.

Visit our website for updates.
www.lawreviewpublishing.com.

TABLE OF CONTENTS

GRAPH 1. COMMON LAW OVERVIEW: CATEGORIES OF CRIMINAL LAW

MENS REA			NATURE OF CRIME		VICTIM		COMPLETION OF ACT		SENTENCE	
Intent		Strict Liability	Mala in Se	Malum Prohibitum	Crimes vs. Property	Crimes vs. Persons	Choate	Inchoate	Misdemeanor	Felony
Specific intent crimes	General intent crimes									
▶ First degree murder	▶ Second degree murder	▶ Felony murder ▶ Statutory rape ▶ Tax evasion ▶ Traffic violations: —moving violations —parking violations (expired meter)	▶ Homicide —murder —manslaughter ▶ Robbery ▶ Rape ▶ Arson	▶ Public nudity ▶ Sodomy ▶ Jaywalking ▶ Littering ▶ Traffic violations: —moving violations —parking violations (expired meter)	▶ Burglary ▶ Arson ▶ Larceny ▶ Embezzlement ▶ Trespass ▶ Nuisance	▶ Homicide —murder —manslaughter ▶ Kidnapping ▶ Rape	▶ Homicide —murder —manslaughter ▶ Robbery ▶ Rape	▶ Solicitation ▶ Conspiracy ▶ Attempt (attempted murder)	▶ Traffic violations: —moving violations (speeding without aggravating circumstances like DUI) —parking violations (expired meter)	▶ Homicide —murder —manslaughter ▶ Robbery ▶ Rape ▶ Arson

Note: For an overview of criminal trial and appellate procedure see *E-Z Review for Criminal Procedure.*

GRAPH 2. HOMICIDE: COMMON LAW ANALYSIS

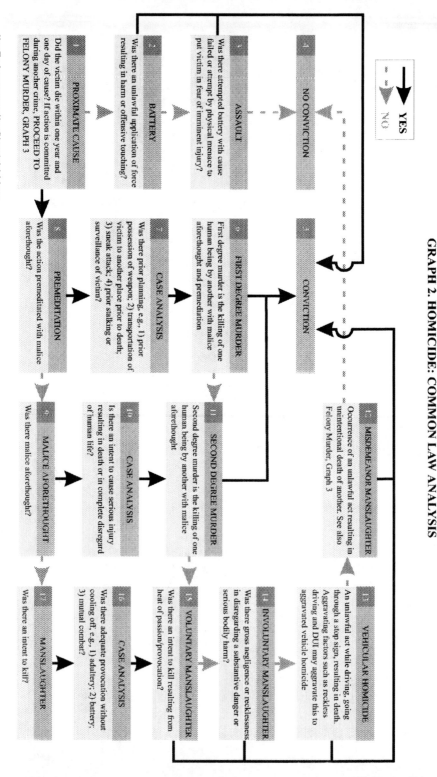

Legend:
- ➤ YES
- ⋯⋯⋯> NO

1 PROXIMATE CAUSE
Did the victim die within one year and one day of cause? If action is committed during another crime, PROCEED TO FELONY MURDER, GRAPH 3

2 BATTERY
Was there an unlawful application of force resulting in harm or offensive touching?

3 ASSAULT
Was there attempted battery with cause failed or attempt by physical menace to put victim in fear of imminent injury?

4 NO CONVICTION

5 CONVICTION

5 PREMEDITATION
Was the action premeditated with malice aforethought?

6 FIRST DEGREE MURDER
First degree murder is the killing of one human being by another with malice aforethought and premeditation

7 CASE ANALYSIS
Was there prior planning, e.g., 1) prior possession of weapon; 2) transportation of victim to another place prior to death; 3) sneak attack; 4) prior stalking or surveillance of victim?

8 MALICE AFORETHOUGHT?

9 MALICE AFORETHOUGHT

10 CASE ANALYSIS
Is there an intent to cause serious injury resulting in death or in complete disregard of human life?

11 SECOND DEGREE MURDER
Second degree murder is the killing of one human being by another with malice aforethought

12 MISDEMEANOR MANSLAUGHTER
Occurrence of an unlawful act resulting in unintentional death of another. See also Felony Murder, Graph 3

13 VEHICULAR HOMICIDE
An unlawful act while driving, going through a stop sign, resulting in death. Aggravating factors such as reckless driving and DUI may aggravate this to aggravated vehicular homicide

14 INVOLUNTARY MANSLAUGHTER
Was there gross negligence or recklessness in disregarding a substantive danger or serious bodily harm?

15 VOLUNTARY MANSLAUGHTER
Was there an intent to kill resulting from heat of passion/provocation?

16 CASE ANALYSIS
Was there adequate provocation without cooling off, e.g., 1) adultery; 2) battery; 3) mutual combat?

17 MANSLAUGHTER
Was there an intent to kill?

Note: The above process considers all lesser-included charges.

GRAPH 3. FELONY MURDER: COMMON LAW ANALYSIS

Legend:
- ➤ YES
- ⟶ NO

1. PROXIMATE CAUSE
Did the victim die within one year and one day of cause?

2. PROCEED TO BOX 2, GRAPH 2

3. CAUSATION & NON-MERGER
Was the killing committed while attempting or committing another crime (non-merger)?

4. DANGEROUSNESS
Is all of the following true: 1) the death was foreseeable; 2) the felony was dangerous; 3) one of the felons directly caused the death?

5. FIRST DEGREE MURDER
The killing occurred while committing or attempting one of the following inherently dangerous crimes: burglary, rape, robbery, arson, kidnapping, felonious escape, deviant sex by threat or force

4. CONVICTION

3. NO CONVICTION

9. INVOLUNTARY MANSLAUGHTER
Is there an unintentional killing resulting from reckless or negligent conduct or from the intentional commission of another crime not a felony?

7. SECOND DEGREE MURDER
The killing occurred while committing or attempting another felony other than those enumerated in First Degree Murder box

10. THIN SKULL RULE
Even if death were not foreseeable, did the victim die because the defendant caused greater injury because he took the victim as he found him?

11. MERGER INTO MURDER
If the act of killing merges into the crime (e.g., child abuse results in death), PROCEED TO GRAPH 2

GRAPH 4. HOMICIDE: MPC ANALYSIS

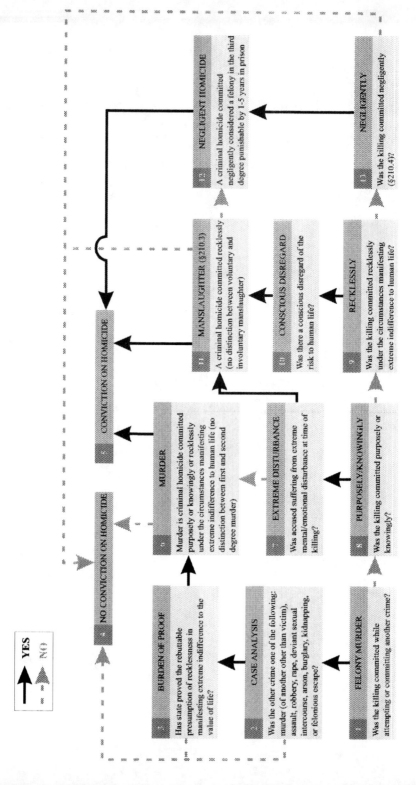

Legend:
- YES (solid arrow)
- NO (dashed arrow)

1 FELONY MURDER
Was the killing committed while attempting or committing another crime?

2 CASE ANALYSIS
Was the other crime one of the following: murder (of another other than victim), assault, robbery, rape, deviant sexual intercourse, arson, burglary, kidnapping, or felonious escape?

3 BURDEN OF PROOF
Has state proved the rebuttable presumption of recklessness in manifesting extreme indifference to the value of life?

4 NO CONVICTION ON HOMICIDE

5 CONVICTION ON HOMICIDE

6 MURDER
Murder is criminal homicide committed purposely or knowingly or recklessly under the circumstances manifesting extreme indifference to human life (no distinction between first and second degree murder)

7 EXTREME DISTURBANCE
Was accused suffering from extreme mental/emotional disturbance at time of killing?

8 PURPOSELY/KNOWINGLY
Was the killing committed purposely or knowingly?

9 RECKLESSLY
Was the killing committed recklessly under the circumstances manifesting extreme indifference to human life?

10 CONSCIOUS DISREGARD
Was there a conscious disregard of the risk to human life?

11 MANSLAUGHTER (§210.3)
A criminal homicide committed recklessly (no distinction between voluntary and involuntary manslaughter)

12 NEGLIGENT HOMICIDE
A criminal homicide committed negligently considered a felony in the third degree punishable by 1-5 years in prison

13 NEGLIGENTLY
Was the killing committed negligently (§210.4)?

GRAPH 5. CRIMES VS. PROPERTY

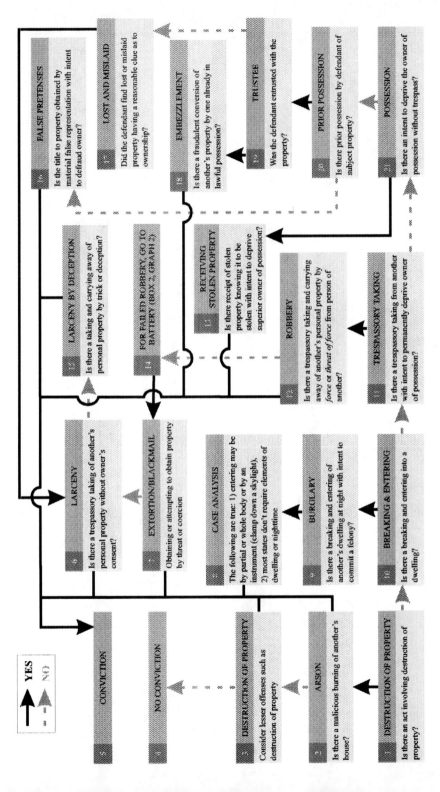

GRAPH 6. EXCUSE DEFENSES

Legend:
- ▶ YES (solid arrow)
- ▷ NO (dashed arrow)

3 EXCULPATING

5 EXCULPATING

4 MPC INSANITY TEST §4.01
Did defendant suffer a mental disease or defect to either 1) appreciate wrongfulness or criminality of the act or 2) ability to conform his actions to the law?

7 IRRESISTIBLE IMPULSE TEST
McNaghten *plus*: 1) substantial inability to control his conduct; *or* 2) could not distinguish between right and wrong

8 DURHAM TEST
Was the crime a product of a mental impairment suffered at time of crime?

9 MCNAGHTEN TEST
Did defendant not know the nature or quality of act or that act was wrong?

10 INSANITY
Is defendant claiming he was insane at time of commission of crime? Analyze the different insanity standards

6 BELOW 7 YEARS
Was the defendant below 7 years old and therefore conclusively presumed to be unable to have a criminal intent?

3 7 TO 14 YEARS
Was the defendant above 7 years old, and below 14 years old, and the prosecutor has *not* overcome the rebuttable presumption of infancy?

2 14 YEARS & OLDER
Was the defendant 14 years or older at the time?

1 INFANCY
Was defendant a non-infant at time of commission of crime?

16 MITIGATING

15 FEDERAL INSANITY TEST
Was the act a result of a *severe* mental defect or disease and defendant was unable to appreciate the nature and quality or wrongfulness of act?

14 DIMINISHED CAPACITY
As a result of a mental defect, was the defendant was incapable of forming specific intent?

13 VOLUNTARY INTOXICATION
Did defendant take intoxicating substance voluntarily?

12 INVOLUNTARY INTOXICATION
Did the defendant take an intoxicating substance unknowingly or under duress, force, or the threat of force?

11 INTOXICATION
Was the defendant intoxicated at time of crime and was intoxication the proximate cause of the crime?

25 NON-EXCULPATING & NON-MITIGATING
PROCEED TO GRAPH 7

24 STRICT LIABILITY
Is the crime charged a strict liability crime such as statutory rape? Defense of mistake of fact or law not applicable

23 CASE ANALYSIS
Is any of the following true: 1) law broken was not published and defendant reasonably relied on statute that was later invalidated; 2) defendant reasonably relied on court decision; 3) defendant reasonably relied on official position to interpret statute (such as Attorney General); 4) statute specifically requires defendant to know act is illegal

22 GENERAL INTENT
Is the crime charged a general intent crime such as second degree murder?

21 REASONABLE MISTAKE
Is it a reasonable mistake of fact?

20 MISTAKE OF LAW
Is defendant raising a mistake of law defense?

19 SPECIFIC INTENT
Is the crime charged a specific intent crime such as first degree murder?

18 UNREASONABLE BUT SINCERE
Is it an unreasonable but sincere mistake of fact?

17 MISTAKE OF FACT
Is defendant raising a mistake of fact defense?

GRAPH 7. JUSTIFICATION DEFENSES

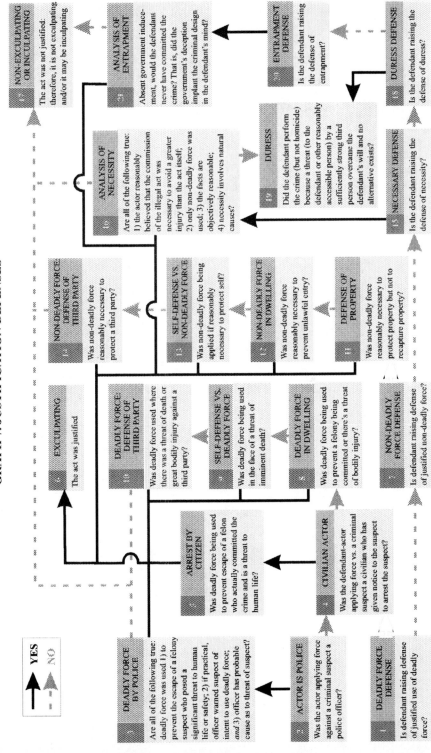

Legend:
- YES (solid arrow)
- NO (dotted arrow)

1. DEADLY FORCE BY POLICE: Are all of the following true: deadly force was used 1) to prevent escape of a felony suspect who posed a significant threat to human life or safety; 2) if practical, officer warned suspect of intent to use deadly force; *and* 3) officer has probable cause as to threat of suspect?

2. ACTOR IS POLICE: Was the actor applying force against a criminal suspect a police officer?

1. DEADLY FORCE DEFENSE: Is defendant raising defense of justified use of deadly force?

5. ARREST BY CITIZEN: Was deadly force being used to prevent escape of a felon who actually committed the crime and is a threat to human life?

4. CIVILIAN ACTOR: Was the defendant-actor applying force vs. a criminal suspect a civilian who has given notice to the suspect to arrest the suspect?

10. DEADLY FORCE: DEFENSE OF THIRD PARTY: Was deadly force used where there was a threat of death or great bodily injury against a third party?

7. SELF-DEFENSE VS. DEADLY FORCE: Was deadly force being used in the face of a threat of imminent death?

8. DEADLY FORCE IN DWELLING: Was deadly force being used to prevent a felony being committed or there's a threat of bodily injury?

3. NON-DEADLY FORCE DEFENSE: Is defendant raising defense of justified non-deadly force?

6. EXCULPATING: The act was justified

14. NON-DEADLY FORCE: DEFENSE OF THIRD PARTY: Was non-deadly force reasonably necessary to protect a third party?

13. SELF-DEFENSE VS. NON-DEADLY FORCE: Was non-deadly force applied if reasonably necessary to protect self?

12. NON-DEADLY FORCE IN DWELLING: Was non-deadly force reasonably necessary to prevent unlawful entry?

11. DEFENSE OF PROPERTY: Was non-deadly force reasonably necessary to protect property but not to recapture property?

9. ANALYSIS OF NECESSITY: Are all of the following true: 1) the actor reasonably believed that the commission of the illegal act was necessary to avoid a greater injury than the act itself; 2) only non-deadly force was used; 3) the facts are objectively reasonable; 4) necessity involves natural causes?

15. NECESSARY DEFENSE: Is the defendant raising the defense of necessity?

19. DURESS: Did the defendant perform the crime (but not homicide) because a threat (to the defendant or other reasonably accessible person) by a sufficiently strong third person overcame the defendant's will and no alternative exists?

18. DURESS DEFENSE: Is the defendant raising the defense of duress?

21. ANALYSIS OF ENTRAPMENT: Absent government inducement, would the defendant never have committed the crime? That is, did the government's deception implant the criminal design in the defendant's mind?

20. ENTRAPMENT DEFENSE: Is the defendant raising the defense of entrapment?

17. NON-EXCULPATING OR INCULPATING: The act was not justified; therefore, it is not exculpating and/or it may be inculpating

I. REASONS FOR PUNISHMENT

A crime is an act committed or omitted (failure to perform a required act) in violation of public law. The "degree" of a crime denotes a particular grade of crime more or less culpable than another grade of the same offense. The classification of offenses is generally provided by statute or Constitution.

A. Deterrence

1. General deterrence
   People are punished in order to instill in non-offenders fear of the consequences of a crime. Deterrence has the following characteristics:

   a. It is less effective for habitual criminal.

   b. It is more effective for first time offender.

   c. It deters members of the public from criminal behavior once they see the consequences suffered by those who commit crimes.

   d. It is forward-looking in the sense of preventing or reducing the incidence of future offensive behavior.

   e. It has a central utilitarian premise that society has the right to take measures that protect its members from harmful behavior. This premise remains widely influential today.

2. Special deterrence
   Special deterrence focuses on the criminal himself and teaches the convict to refrain from crime by instilling in him a fear of punishment by society.

   a. Special deterrence refers to steps taken to discourage individual offenders from repeating their misconduct

   b. This theory presupposes that the actor who offends once may desire to commit future violations, but assumes that the costs imposed by the past punishment will deter offenders from repeating their misconduct.

3. Theories of deterrence

    a. There is uncertainty in being caught and of actually receiving punishment commensurate with the crime.

    b. There is a delay in implementing justice and punishment.

    c. There is general Ignorance of both the law and punishment in the general population, which makes deterrence difficult.

B. Incapacitation

The goal of incapacitation is to get the person off the street so he cannot commit any more crimes and has the following characteristics:

1. It deprives criminals of their liberty by imprisonment and ends their ability to commit offenses against other citizens.

2. It should be used only in cases where it is needed to restrain the offender from committing a future offense.

3. It requires the system to develop a mechanism that distinguishes those offenders who are potentially recidivist from those who are not.

4. It is founded on offender-based policies, which extend the time served for those predicted to be high-rate offenders among all those convicted of the same charge and use charge-based policies which impose mandatory minimum terms on all offenders convicted of selected offense types in which high-rate offenders tend to engage.

C. Theory of Retribution

The theory of retribution presupposes that human actors are responsible moral agents who are capable of making choices for good and evil. Therefore it is right to punish one who offends against societal norms because it is wrong to violate those norms. By attributing misconduct to offenders' choices - rather than to their impoverished circumstances - retributive theory allows the community to avoid its responsibility for poverty and related cultural ills based on the following principles:

1. Revenge means an eye for an eye and a tooth for a tooth.

2. Atonement is morally centered. The criminal must repay his debt to society by providing something in kind in return. One atones for moral sin by surrendering liberty.

D. Rehabilitation.   Rehabilitation helps people reintegrate back into society.

II. MENS REA

A. The Historical Origins of Mens Rea

Regina v. Faulkner, 13 Cox C.C. 550 (Ireland 1877)
Facts: Defendant set fire to a ship when he lit a match to see how to lug a hole he had put in a rum cask to steal alcohol. He was indicted for arson though he had no intention to set the fire and was not alleged to have acted recklessly or negligently. He was tried under a theory of transferred intent. That is, his intent to commit larceny translates into intent to commit arson to satisfy the mental state requirement.
Issue: Did the trial court err in accepting the prosecution's jury instructions based on transferred intent?
Holding: The court held yes. Defendant did not intend to set the fire, but it might have been a necessary or probable consequence of his actions. If the offense was a probable consequence, he would have foreseen or ought to have foreseen the consequences. The prosecutor insisted that Defendant be found criminally responsible for every result arising from his theft, even if such results could not have been foreseen. No authority in the law supports such an extensive proposition. Defendant's intent was to commit larceny. This is evidence of malice in general. His intent to commit larceny might have been sufficiently connected to the act of arson, if the jury had found that the injury was a reasonable consequence of the larceny. Without such a finding, the conviction cannot be sustained.

B. The evolution of mens rea

1. A guilty mind, or *mens rea* is generally regarded as an essential requirement for the imposition of criminal liability.

2. It is coming to mean today, not so much a mind bent on evil-doing as an intent to do that which unduly endangers social or public interests.

Morissette v. United States, 342 U.S. 246 (1952)
Facts: The defendant came across an apparently abandoned pile of bomb casings while hunting on an Air Force practice bombing range. Defendant took three tons of casings to his farm and flattened them with his tractor. He sold the casing for $84. He was indicted and charged with having stolen property of the United States. Defendant argued that he had acted with innocent intention.
Issue: Is there an implied mental state element in the definition of knowing conversion under which Defendant was charged?
Holding: Yes. The default rule states that when a crime originates in common law, a mental state must be implied if the statute codifies common law.
Reasoning:

  i. To interpret a statute as having no criminal intent goes against the construction of all criminal statutes.

  ii Conversion is not silent because of the word knowingly. It is only unclear as to what word knowingly modifies.

C. The tradition of mens rea

1. Generally speaking, larceny and other theft crimes require an intent to steal, which is an intent to effect a permanent deprivation of property.

2. There are two types of intent under the common law culpability structure:

    a. Specific Intent: the social purposes of those crimes were not implicated unless the offender had the particular state of mind included in the definition of the crime.

    b. General intent: described in its application to specific exculpatory defenses, which tend to change its meaning based on policies that govern the availability and scope of different defenses.

3. If the offense required a general intent, then a mistake of fact was a defense only if it was honest and reasonable, but if the offense required a specific intent, then a mistake of fact was a defense if honestly made, whether or not it was reasonable under the circumstances.

D. Culpability

1. Definition

   The term *"mens rea"* requires that there be called a "culpable state of mind."

   Not state of mind in all cases
   In most situations, the requirement of *mens rea* refers to what we would all agree is a mental state. But some crimes are defined in such a way that the *mens rea* is merely "negligence" or "recklessness". In these cases it is often stretching it to say that there is a particular state of mind involved at all. Rather the state of mind is based on the reasonable person standard.

2. Model Penal Code ("MPC") on culpability

   The MPC, as have many statutes, has done away with the distinction of general and specific intent in lieu of *"purposely, knowingly, and recklessly."*

   Specific intent corresponds roughly to purpose/knowledge and general intent corresponds roughly to recklessness/ negligence.

   MPC is based on the proposition that four culpability concepts are both necessary and sufficient to define criminal offenses:
   a. purpose,
   b. knowledge,
   c. recklessness, and
   d. negligence.

   The *mens rea* elements of a given crime are determined by ascertaining which of these four terms applies to each of the *actus-reus* components of the offense and by adding any other specifically defined *mens rea* requirement.

   Once a crime is broken down into its conduct, circumstance, and result components, one of the four culpability concepts will be applied to each component in order to determine the level of *mens rea* required for that offense.

3. Four culpability concepts

    a. <u>Purposely</u>
        i.   Definition.   The positive desire or conscious objective to engage in the particular conduct in question.
        ii. Transferred intent. This principle seems to contradict case law in that if one desires to produce one result, his intent will be transferred over to another, unexpected result that happens.
        iii. Conditional intent. The principle that a person desires a result but only on the happening of another condition does not usually negate the intent for the result. For example: The defendant breaks into a house to commit burglary only on the condition that no one is home. This condition does not negate the intent for burglary.

    b. <u>Knowingly</u>
       The actor acts knowingly if he is conscious that his conduct is of a certain kind or value, or that certain known circumstances exist. He acts knowingly as to the result if he is *implicitly certain* that his conduct will cause that result.

    c. <u>Recklessly</u>
       A person acts recklessly when he consciously disregards a substantial and unjustifiable risk to be aware of the risk. The MPC applies a subjective standard.
        i.   All the surrounding circumstances are considered when determining if the risk was substantial and unjustifiable, such as motive.
        ii. For example, the defendant is driving very fast: is he trying to get to the hospital or is he joy riding?

    d. <u>Negligently</u>
       A person acts negligently when he should be aware of a substantial and unjustifiable risk.
        i.   This is an objective standard. Thus, if a reasonable person is aware of the risk, the defendant should be too.
        ii. The MPC holds that criminal liability should be imposed only if *gross negligence* is present. That is, only if there is a *gross deviation* from the standard of care that a reasonable person would observe.

NOTE:

A) Where the crime is *not* defined in precision, the MPC states that the default *mens rea* is recklessness. Further, as long as you have a higher *mens rea* than the statute requires, you can still be convicted of the crime.

B) If a culpability level is assigned to an offense without distinguishing among elements, that level applies to all material elements of the offense.

C) If culpability other than negligence is established; all lower levels of culpability are also established, *a fortiori*.

D) MPC §2.02(3): "where the culpability sufficient to establish a material element of an offense is not prescribed by law, such element is established if a person acts *purposely, knowingly, or recklessly with* respect thereto." That is, since recklessness is default, if defendant acts with recklessness or anything higher, he has the requisite *mens rea*.

---

4. Ambiguity: Ambiguous vs. Unambiguous.
   Most crimes have a number of material elements, each of which the prosecution is required to prove usually beyond a reasonable doubt. In many cases, the mental state required for each of these material elements may not be the same.

   a. MPC §2.02
      Comment: The problem of the kind of culpability that is required for conviction must be faced separately with respect to each material element of the offense, although the answer in many cases is the same with respect to each element.

   b. Ambiguous vs. Unambiguous under MPC

      i. If a statute is ambiguous on its face, the *mens rea* attaches to all the material elements of the statute *unless* a contrary purpose clearly appears (MPC § 2.02 (4)).

      ii. If a statute is unambiguous on its face, the mens rea attaches to the material elements of the statute specifically stated. The other remaining elements are called *objective elements* and they do not have a *mens rea* element attached to them. The objective elements are strict liability elements and they merely need to be proved to exist.

c.   If a statute has no *mens rea* stated, then the *mens rea* of recklessness is used as a default. Thereafter, recklessness attaches to all of the material elements. Objective elements, as before, do not have a *mens rea* element attached.

d.   Clearly the prosecutor will try to say that as many elements as possible in the statute do not need a *mens rea* element and therefore are objective elements.

Carter v. United States, No.99-5716 (June 12, 2000).

Facts: Carter, wearing a ski mask, confronted a bank customer outside of the bank and pushed her back into the bank. Cater jumped over the counter and the teller ran into a manager's office. Carter took the opportunity to remove the money from the money drawers. Carter was later apprehended and charged with 18 U. S. C. §2113(a), which punishes "[w]hoever, by force and violence, or by intimidation, takes . . . any . . . thing of value [from a] bank." Carter pleaded not guilty. His legal argument was that he had not taken the bank's money "by force and violence, or by intimidation," as §2113(a) requires. Prior to trial, he moved for a jury instruction on the offense described by §2113(b) as a lesser-included offense of the offense described by §2113(a). Section 2113(b) entails less severe penalties than §2113(a), punishing, inter alia, "[w]hoever takes and carries away, with intent to steal or purloin, any . . . thing of value exceeding $1,000 [from a] . . . bank." The prosecution argued that there are two different levels of intent between (a) and (b), general and specific. The District Court denied Carter's motion. The jury, instructed on §2113(a) alone, returned a guilty verdict, pursuant to which the District Court entered judgment. Carter appealed to the Third Circuit, however, the Third Circuit affirmed.

Held: The Supreme Court affirmed. The Court held that because §2113(b) requires three elements not mandated by §2113(a), it is not a lesser-included offense of §2113(a), and Carter is prohibited from obtaining a lesser-included offense instruction on the offense described by §2113(b).

5. Willfully
    The MPC states that for a person to act willfully, it is not necessary that he act purposefully. Knowingly is sufficient.
    For example: The law purports it is murder to willfully take another person's life. For example, if the defendant brings a bomb on a boat to kill passenger X, the defendant is guilty of the murders of both X and Y because he is practically certain that his action will kill Y, even though Y is not the intended victim.

6. Subjective Standard
    A person's knowledge is whether *he actually* knew or believed something, not merely whether a reasonable person in the position of the defendant would have had that information or opinion.

7. Willful Disregard
    This exception to the knowledge rule states that if a defendant has a suspicion that something is the case, but in order to be able to deny knowledge, has purposely refrained from pursuing an investigation that would have led to the information in question, he cannot claim that he does not have the knowledge.

EXAMPLE: Noriego comes across the border driving a gasoline truck with drugs in the tank. Noriego knew of the tank but says he did not look into the tank because he did not want to know. He cannot escape liability this way.

E. Mens Rea, Ignorance, Mistake of Criminality and Mistake of Fact

A mistake of law or mistake of fact is an affirmative defense that is raised by the defendant. It will prevail as an affirmative defense if it negates the *mens rea* of the statute.

1. Affirmative Defenses
    The prosecution is required to prove every element beyond a reasonable doubt. An affirmative defense will allow a defendant to exonerate himself notwithstanding the fact that the prosecution proves the crime beyond a reasonable doubt.

2. Burdens in an affirmative defense

    There are two burdens:

    a. Burden-of-Production
        Defense always has the burden of production for an affirmative defense. Therefore, if the defendant does not present the evidence, it is assumed that he waives the affirmative defense.

    b. Burden-of-Persuasion
        If an affirmative defense goes to the *mens rea* of an element of the crime proven by the prosecution, then in this circumstance the defense is responsible for the burden of persuading jury or trier of fact that the defense is valid by a preponderance of the evidence.

NOTE: The prosecution must convince the trier of fact "beyond a reasonable doubt."

---

3. Ignorance or Mistake of Criminality. A mistake of law is considered conceptually distinct from a mistake of fact, and has a different exculpatory effect. In general, ignorance of the law is no excuse.

    a. Mistake of Law.

State v. Fox, 866 P.2d 181 (Idaho 1993)

Facts: Fox ordered 100,000 tablets of ephedrine from an out-of-state mail order distributor. In some states ephedrine is a legal over-the-counter drug, and in others, illegal.

Issue: Did the district court err in holding that mistakes of law are not defenses to the crime of possession of a controlled substance?

Holding: No. The *mens rea* element of the offense of possession of a controlled substance is knowledge of possession, not knowledge that the substance possessed is a controlled substance.

> b. Reliance on Local Authority.

Hopkins v. State, 69 A.2d 456 (Md. 1950)

Facts: Hopkins checked with local states attorney to determine if certain signs violated an anti-sign law. He was later convicted for using signs that had been approved.

Issue: Should Hopkins be held criminally liable even though he checked with public officials regarding the legality of the signs?

Holding: Yes. A person who commits an act which the law declares to be criminal cannot be excused from punishment upon the theory that he misunderstood the law. The fact that the state's attorney confirmed the misconstruction was thought inconsequential.

> c. Holding of a Lower Court as a Defense.

State v. Striggles, 210 N.W. 137 (Iowa 1926)

Facts: A municipal court held that a machine was not a gambling device. When the Supreme Court of Iowa held that the device was illegal, Defendant was convicted.

Issue: Should Defendant be held criminally liable even though his actions were based on the decision of a municipal court?

Holding: Yes. The court refused to hold that the decisions of any court below, inferior to the Supreme Court, were available as a defense under similar circumstances.

4. Ignorance is an excuse -- The Exception

Lambert v. California, 355 U.S. 225 (1957)

Facts: Defendant was a convicted felon living in Los Angeles. She did not register with the state as a convicted felon and was fined.
Issue: Should Defendant be held criminally liable for not registering with the state, even though she had no reason to know that she should register?

Holding: No. Although this is a mistake of law, she was not doing anything and therefore had no reason to know and was not on notice that she should register.

NOTE:

i.	*Lambert* is rarely applied and is always distinguished.
ii.	In some cases, there is a due process exception (notice) to ignorance of the law is no excuse.
iii.	In *Lambert,* there is a concern about trapping innocent people.

5. Ignorance is a statutory excuse in some jurisdictions:

Cox v. Louisiana, 379 U.S. 559 (1965)

Facts: Picketers were told that 101 feet from the courthouse was not "near the courthouse" but the picketers were subsequently arrested.
Issue: Should the defendants be held liable even though they were told that they were not breaking the law?

Holding: No. To allow them to be convicted would sanction an indefensible sort of entrapment by the state.

6. Mistake of Law - Theories
    a. Support for mistake of law as a defense
       i. The threat of penal sanctions can have a deterrent effect if the actor reasonably believes his conduct is lawful.
       ii. Mistake of law is a general deterrent effect.

b.   Opposition to mistake of law as a defense

     i.   Everyone has an innate sense of right and wrong, and in that sense everyone can be presumed to know the law.

     ii.   It would be infeasible from an implementation standpoint to admit ignorance of the law as a defense. It would be nearly impossible and a significant burden on the courts to decide the necessary questions:

     A)   Was the party ignorant?

     B)   Was her ignorance inevitable?

     iii.   Beyond practical difficulties, ignorance of the law should not be admitted for substantive reasons. To admit the excuse at all would be to encourage ignorance where the law-maker has determined to make men know and obey. Justice to the individual is rightly outweighed by the larger interests of society.

     iv.   If the defense of ignorance of the law were admitted, "whenever a defendant in a criminal case thought the law was thus and so, he is to be treated as though the law were thus and so, i.e., the law actually is thus and so it opposes objectivity to subjectivity."

7.   MPC § 2.04 Ignorance

Ignorance or mistake as matter of fact or law is a defense only when:

a.   It negates the purpose.

b.   It is defensible

The common law provides that a state of mind established by such ignorance or mistake constitutes a defense

c.   Exception under MPC to mistake of criminal law claim under §2.04(3)(a) - the statute or other enactment defining the offense is not known to the actor and has not been published or otherwise reasonably made available prior to the conduct alleged.

d. Ignorance as a Defense is Allowed
  i. First, What is the *mens rea* as enumerated by the statute? Isolate the culpability level in the law.
  ii. Second,
      What is the affirmative defense that is raised?
      An affirmative defense of *mistake or ignorance of the law* is allowed only if it negates the *mens rea* of the crime.

EXAMPLE 1. A defendant was charged with trafficking in counterfeit art. The statute read "guilty if *intentionally trafficking and knowingly using a counterfeit art*". The defendant raises the affirmative defense of "ignorance of the law."

  A) What is the *mens rea*? Intentionally.
  B) What is the affirmative defense? Ignorance.
  C) Does the defense negate the *mens rea* of the crime? No, the person intentionally transported the material, he is only ignorant that it was illegal.
  D) Thus, he cannot use the defense.

EXAMPLE 2. In the case where the IRS agent murdered the tax cheater, the defendant claimed mistake of law.

Here, the defense does not go to the *mens rea* of the crime. He was not ignorant that he was killing the cheater. Therefore, the affirmative defense is not successful. (c) Example 3: Mozart is caught smuggling 14 cocaine plants. A statute making it a felony to knowingly possess 100 kg of cocaine- "knowingly" applies to the weight as well as the nature of the drug.

  A) Since there was no way for the defendant to know the cocaine weight in the cocaine leaves was over 100 kg because there was no standard correlation between this weight and the cocaine weight, he could not be convicted under the statute.
  B) There is no discernible legislative intent to make the weight of a drug a strict liability element.

---

    e.   Ignorance of Law as Excuse in Strict Liability Crimes.

State v. Hatch, 313 A.2d 797 (N.J. 1973).

Holding: The court held that a defendant's lack of knowledge of the law can never be held as a defense in a strict liability crime.

        i.   Defendant was prosecuted for not encasing his guns when he came into NJ. He claimed mistake of law because Massachusetts, his home state, did not require this. The court rejected the argument.

        ii.   This was a commission to act. To prove the prosecutor must show that:

            A) There was a duty to act;

            B) The defendant was aware of the duty;

            C) The act was committed.

    8.   Mistakes of Non-Criminal Law

        a.   Honest Belief of Mistakes of Criminal Law

State v. Woods, 179 A. 1 (Vt. 1935)

Facts: Defendant was arrested under the "Blanket Act" for sleeping with another woman's husband. She contended that an honest belief that the man she married was divorced and her marriage was valid should be a defense.

Issue: Should Defendant be able to argue that she did not have the required *mens rea* because she misunderstood non-criminal law essential to her criminal liability?

Holding: No. Mistake of non-criminal law is not a defense in this case. The holding seems to suggest that the required *mens rea* for the Blanket Act is general intent.

b. On Mistakes of Non-Criminal Law

   i. The situation arises when Defendant makes a mistake of non-criminal law relevant to the criminality of conduct.

   ii. If Defendant makes a mistake as to the relevant law of property and wrongly comes to the conclusion that she or he owns certain property, is it a defense if the actor then does things with or to the property that would otherwise constitute larceny or burglary?

   iii. Under Common Law, if the offense required a specific intent or some other special mental element, a mistake of the non-criminal law that negated the required *mens rea* was a defense.

   iv. Under common law no mistakes of law were exculpatory for general intent crimes.

9. Mistake of Fact in Common Law

   a. If mistake of fact is honest, this is exculpatory in specific intent cases.
   b. If mistake of fact is honest and reasonable, this is exculpatory in general intent cases.

   i. Must read mistake of fact cases to determine culpability of common law offenses.
   ii. General intent is the default category - if statute or cases have no particular intent attached, it's general intent.

III. STRICT LIABILITY

A. Strict Liability Distinguished from Mens Rea

1. *Mens Rea* Requirement
    Most common law crimes are defined so that they are committed if only the defendant acted *intentionally, knowingly, recklessly,* or at least *negligently.*

    a. Types of Crimes
        The types of crimes that need a *mens rea* requirement are usually crimes against persons (ex: murder, assault, rape) or crimes against property (ex: theft, burglary, larceny).

    b. Crimes that are punishable by incarceration usually include a *mens rea* requirement. This is because the state does not want to imprison someone unless they had the specific intention to do the offense.

2. Crimes requiring *no culpability* are called strict liability crimes:

    a. Many of the regulatory or public welfare violations are strict liability crimes because of the risk to the public that the crimes pose, because they involve morality or because they are especially dangerous.

    b. They usually only carry a fine and usually no jail time, except in a few extreme cases, (ex: Statutory Rape).

    c. Types of crimes:
        i.   OSHA regulations;
        ii.   Statutory Rape;
        iii. Automobile violations;
        iv.   Mislabeling/mishandling of drugs;
        v.   Environmental statutes.

B. Interpretation

1. When is Strict Imposed?
   The legislature does not usually delineate when strict liability is to be imposed. The statutes are sometimes old and vague and fail to specify a *mens rea* requirement even where one is intended.

2. Rules
   The Court lists the following rules for interpretation to resolve the nature of the violation:

   a. The infractions concern neglect or inaction, rather than pro-active aggression.

   b. No direct injury to person or property, but simply a danger of such, and it is this danger that the statute seeks to avoid.

   c. The penalty imposed is small, usually fines.

   d. Little danger to the defendant's reputation within the community.

3. Cases

   a. Lack of Knowledge of Underlying Facts.

People v. Hutchinson, 400 N.Y.S. 2d 340 (N.Y. App. Div. 1977)

Holding: The court held that the defendant could not be convicted of a strict liability offense without some knowledge of the underlying facts.

   b. Vicarious Liability for Criminal Activity

U.S. v. Park, 421 U.S. 658 (1975)

Holding: The court held that the defendant, President of the company, was liable for adulator Acme shipments because he was in the best position to affect change.

> **NOTE: EXCEPTION.** The court propounded an *exception so* that the President of a company will not be required to do the impossible. Thus, if he was *powerless* to effect the change or was new on the job, he was not the *responsible party*.

> **NOTE:** The MPC rejects incarceration of a company president for violations.

c.   Extremely Dangerous Crimes.

United States v. Freed, 401 U.S. 601 (1971)
Facts: Defendant was held strictly liable for possessing unregistered hand grenades.
Issue: Can Defendant be convicted on a strict liability *mens rea* for possessing unregistered hand grenades?
Holding: Yes. The case involves extremely dangerous items which makes us more willing to dispense with *mens rea*.

> **NOTE:** Freed must know that he possessed hand grenades. The Supreme Court accepts strict liability for some elements and *mens rea* for others - Punishment is appropriate even though knowledge of wrongdoing is wanting.

4.   Special requirement under the MPC

    a.   Material Elements
Under the MPC § 1.04(5), if strict liability is imposed as to *any material element* of an offense, the offense can only be a *"violation."*
A violation under the code is a minor offense that does not constitute a crime and that may be punished only by fine or forfeiture.

b.   Narrowly Defined
The MPC suggests for application to non-Code statutes that these statutes will be purported to impose strict liability only insofar as a legislature purpose to impose strict liability.   In other words, Congressional silence does not equal strict liability.

C. Strict Liability Crimes Against People

1.   Statutory Rape
The defendant is guilty if he has intercourse with a person below a prescribed age whether or not he knew or should have known the true age. This is true even if the child looks of age and lies about the age. *See Regina v. Prince, infra.*

Regina v. Prince, L.R. 2 C.C.R. 154 (1875)

Holding: The court held that when a defendant took a girl who was under age 16 years old away from her father and against his will, the fact that he believed her to be over 18 years old did not matter (she lied about her age).

a.   Assume that the *mens rea* applies to each element unless otherwise stated.

b.   If a statute does not make *mens rea* an element of a crime, knowledge of the pertinent facts does not matter.

2.   Bigamy
This is the crime of being married to two or more persons at one time.

IV.   THE REQUIREMENT OF AN ACT

A.   Actus Reus

1. Requirements.
   a.   Actus reus requires an overt voluntary act.
   b.   Requirement of Overt Illegal Act.

Proctor v. State, 176 P. 771 (Okla. Crim. App. 1918)

Holding: The court held that a criminal conviction requires an overt illegal act.   Mere "guilty" thoughts or criminal intent alone are insufficient to convict a person.

   i.   Inference allowed
        Possession shifts burden to defendant to explain possession of a large quantity of liquor.
   ii. Standard
        A rational connection between fact being inferred and fact being proven. A permissive presumption which will be *rebutted* by defendant.

   c.   Thoughts alone are insufficient. Thoughts coupled with an overt act are actionable.

   d.   The act elements of the offense are characterized as conduct, circumstances and results.

      i.   Conduct elements describe the acts or omissions required to commit an offense. Every offense must contain some conduct as so defined although sometimes the exact nature of the conduct is not described.
      ii. Circumstance elements consist of external facts that must exist in order for the crime to be committed (personal property of another).
      iii. Result elements are any consequence of Defendant's conduct that are incorporated in the definition of the offense.
      iv. Most offenses are defined only in terms of conduct and circumstances with no required result.

23

2. Significance
   a. Defendant has not committed physical acts, but has guilty words, thoughts or innuendo or status in the community (ex: drug user).
   b. Involuntary act.
   c. Omission, or failure to act.
   d. Defining Acts and Due Process.

Keeler v. Superior Court of Amador County, 470 P.2d 617 (Ca. 1970)

Facts: Defendant attacked his estranged wife, who was pregnant with another man's child, and kicked her abdomen. She went to the hospital where the fetus was stillborn. Defendant was brought up on murder charges.

Issue: Is an unborn but viable fetus a human being within the meaning of the CA statute defining murder?

Holding: No. The court supported the view held in *Chavez* that "a viable child in the process of being born" is a human being within the meaning of the homicide statutes, whether or not the process has been fully completed. In this case, the fetus was not in the process of being born. Keeler relies on the common law definition of human being as born alive. On the other hand, the state argues that if life can be extended one way in the life spectrum, why can it not be extended the other way? Canon of Strict Construction. The words of the statute should be construed as favorably as possible to the accused. Court did not want to find Keeler guilty because they could be violating his due process rights. Keeler had no notice of a new definition of what a human being is.

24

e.   Common Social Duty as Due Notice.

People v. Sobiek, 106 Cal. Rptr. 519 (Ca. Ct. App. 1973)

Facts: Defendant and 14 friends organized an Empire Investment Group to invest money in second mortgages. Defendant was elected president. Defendant gradually assumed practically unlimited control of the making of loans and finally appropriated to his own use considerable sums of the group's money.

Issue: By appropriating partnership money for his own use, was Defendant stealing the property of another?

Holding: Yes. Common social duty would have forewarned Defendant that circumspect conduct prohibited robbing his partners and also would have told him that he was stealing the property of another.

3.   The Requirement of Previously Defined Conduct

Kolender v. Lawson, 461 U.S. 352 (1983)

Facts: Defendant had been stopped 15 times previously by CA police and files a civil suit that declaration 647(e) is void for vagueness.

Issue: Is the credible and reliable ID element of the statute void for vagueness?

Holding: The Supreme Court says yes. Statute 647(e) is unconstitutionally vague on its face because it encourages arbitrary enforcement by failing to describe with sufficient particularity what a suspect must do in order to satisfy the statute.

4.   Crime (Act) or sentencing factor.
     The legislature mandates what is a crime and what the sentencing is for violation of that crime. However, in many instances, the courts have confused the two especially in the realm of mandatory sentences.

Castillo v. United States, No. 99-658 (June 5, 2000)

Facts: Defendants were arrested and indicted for conspiring to murder federal officers. The defendants were charged under 18 U.S.C. §924(c)(1) which reads in relevant part: "Whoever, during and in relation to any crime of violence . . . uses or carries a firearm, shall, in addition to the punishment provided for such crime . . . be sentenced to imprisonment for five years . . . and if the firearm is [for example] a machinegun . . . to imprisonment for thirty years." The jury found the defendants guilty. At sentencing, the judge found that the firearms included machineguns and imposed the mandatory 30-year prison sentence. The defendants appealed to the Fifth Circuit. The Fifth Circuit affirmed, concluding that statutory words such as "machinegun" create sentencing factors, not elements of a separate crime.

Holding: The Supreme Court reversed and remanded. The Court indicated that Section 924(c)(1) uses the word "machinegun" (and similar words) to state an element of a separate, aggravated crime. The Court set forth three reasons for their ruling. First, the Court noted that while the statute's literal language appears neutral, the statute's overall construction strongly favors a "new crime" interpretation. The Court opined that the first sentence of §924(c)(1) clearly establishes the elements of the basic federal offense of using or carrying a gun during a crime of violence, and specifically that Congress placed that component and the word machinegun in a single sentence. The Court articulated that, in addition, the next three sentences refer directly to sentencing. The Court opined that this strongly suggests that the entire first sentence defines crimes. Second, the Supreme Court noted that courts, in general, have not used firearm categories (such as "machinegun") as sentencing factors where the use or carrying of the firearm is itself the substantive crime. Third, the Court noted that to have a jury of peers, rather than a lone judge, to decide whether a defendant used or carried a machinegun would not complicate a trial or risk prejudice/unfairness. Fourth, the Court stated that the legislative history favors interpreting §924(c) as setting forth elements rather than sentencing factors. Finally, the Court set forth that the duration and severity of an added mandatory sentence that turns on the presence or absence of a "machinegun" (or any of the other listed firearm types) weighs in favor of treating such offense-related words as referring to an element in this context.

B. Vagueness Doctrine

1. **Definition.** Vagueness is the failure to give notice to ordinary people, in violation of their due process rights.

2. As applied vs. facial challenge. In an "as applied" challenge" in Lawson, there is no vagueness. But in a facial challenge, one can imagine cases where we would not know what satisfies this statute.

3. Lawson gets to make a facial challenge because underlying it are constitutional rights

   a. Right to Movement; and

   b. First Amendment liberties.

4. A vague statute on the books could create a chilling effect, creating a large gray area that some people will not enter. Therefore, their constitutional rights are violated.

5. The rationales of the vagueness doctrine are as follows:

   a. A vague statute fails to give adequate notice of what is prohibited.

   b. An indefinite law invites arbitrary and discriminatory enforcement. In essence, the power to define a vague state is left to those who enforce it.

6. The following are limitations on the vagueness doctrine:

   a. There is something inescapably fictive about the notion that potential criminals learn what is forbidden from the words of a statute.

   b. The precision required of a penal statute need not appear on the face.

C. Actus Reus Distinguished

Mere thoughts are never punishable as crimes. Likewise, words alone are not punishable as crimes (with few exceptions).

1. <u>Confession is not Enough</u>
    Even if defendant has confessed (words) his evil intentions to a third party this will usually not be enough to constitute an *actus reus*. However, if a person confesses to a crime (murder) and the police know the murder was committed with a .38 caliber handgun and the defendant produces a recently discharged .38 caliber gun, this could be enough. *See Possession supra.*

2. <u>Need More than Words</u>
    In many jurisdictions, an agreement between two persons to commit a crime is a sufficient act to commit conspiracy as long as there is an act in furtherance of that goal. For example, Richie and Ralph agree to kill Potsie (not a crime). However, the next day they buy a long scope rifle. This could be the act.

3. <u>Possession</u>
    Possession of an object could establish the necessary criminal act. For instance, possession of a concealed weapon is a crime.
    a. Normally, the act of possession is construed as conscious possession that is with knowledge.

    b. Knowledge of the guilty nature of the item is not necessary. Nor is it necessary that the possessor know of the item's illegal or contraband nature.

    c. Possession may be thought of as a status that begins with the act of acquisition and that is continued by a failure to divest.

    d. Possession is an act, that is, the possessor knowingly procured or received the thing possessed or was aware of his control thereof for a sufficient period to have been able to terminate his possession.

4. Conspiracy

   a. *Mens rea* means that the objective/purpose of the defendant is to carry out the crime

   b. Overt act. If there is no overt act, the state may fall back on the common law definition where no overt act is required.

   c. How does agreement get proved in practice?

      i. **Audio tapes, written documents, testimony**

      ii. Need evidence of an implicit agreement

      iii Behavior, concerted action, part of a prearranged plan

   d. Overt act need not be criminal.

   e. Do not have to finish completed crime to be convicted (inchoate crime).

      i. **Pinkerton Rule**

      ii. Is other crime a reasonably foreseeable and natural consequence?

5. Control
In order to be in possession, the defendant must not only be aware of the contraband's presence, but must have control over them.

6. MPC §2.01(4)

   a. Possession can be a criminal act only if the defendant knew he had possession of the object; AND

   b. Defendant was aware of his control thereof for a sufficient period to have been able to terminate his possession.

7. Presumptions
Proof of possession is usually easier for the state to prove because of statutory presumptions in which the statute automatically presumes possession for certain types of contraband.

D. Status Not Enough

A person cannot be convicted for merely having a certain status or condition. There must be an illegal act. For example, the status of being a cocaine addict is not a crime.

1.   Voluntary Acts

        a.   Act must be voluntary.

        b.   Something more than words.

        c.   In some instances it can be an omission to act.

2.   Cases

        a.   Involuntary Acts.

Martin v. State, 17 So. 2d 427 (Ala. Ct. App. 1944)
Holding: The police dragged a drunkard from his house into the street for an arrest. The defendant was convicted of public drunkenness. The court held the public drunkenness was involuntary. Thus, no crime.

        b.   Knowledge and Voluntariness of Act.

People v. Grant, 360 N.E. 2d 809 (1977)
Holding: The court reversed the trial court because of the lack of an involuntary instruction. The court remanded for finding on remand, if the defendant:
      i.   knew of his epileptic condition;
      ii.   knew that alcohol brought on a seizure; and
      iii .   voluntarily drank the alcohol.

If the answer is yes to all of the above, then the requirements for an *actus reus* may be fulfilled and the defendant is guilty.

c.   Seizure as Incapacitation of Liability.

People v. Decina, 138 N.E.2d 799 (N.Y. 1956)

Facts: Decina has epileptic seizure while driving and kills several children.

Issue: Does the fact that the seizure incapacitates (involuntary) excuse criminal liability?

Holding: No. Because Defendant decided to drive when he knew he could have a seizure makes him liable. The penal code only requires conduct that includes a voluntary act. The voluntary act was driving the car.

d.   Mere Condition or Status as Addict vs. Overt Act.

Robinson v. California, 370 U.S. 660 (1962).

1.   Criminal liability requires an act, omission, or possession and cannot be based on a mere condition or status.
2.   One cannot be convicted for being addicted to narcotics.
3.   A broader interpretation of the case focuses on voluntariness and possibility of decriminalizing addictive behavior.

e.   Status of Alcoholism Does not Negate Voluntariness.

Powell v. Texas, 392 U.S. 514 (1968)

Facts: Powell tried to plead the same facts as *Robinson* when prosecuted for intoxication in a public place. He tried to show that as an alcoholic, his behavior was "involuntary".

Holding: The court rejected this argument and restricted *Robinson* to be only concerned with conviction based on status or condition.
Notions of voluntariness are left to the state legislatures and courts. If you enter into a conspiracy and crimes are carried out, each person in conspiracy can be held accountable for all crimes even though they did not commit them.

3. MPC §2.01(2)
   The following are involuntary acts and cannot satisfy the *actus reus* requirement under any circumstances.

   a. Reflex or Involuntary Movement
      i. A reflex act or involuntary bodily movement does not give rise to criminal liability because it is involuntary. It is not a voluntary act of the person.
      ii. A quick but conscious decision is not considered reflexive as long as defendant has time to make some decision as whether to take that action. For example, a person walking on the train, the train shifts tracks and knocks the person off balance, the person reaches out grabs the breast of a woman in hopes of regaining balance. The person is not guilty of sexual assault, assault, battery or sexual battery.

   b. Unconsciousness or Sleep
      i. Automatism
         An act performed when unconscious is always involuntary.
      ii. Person must prove at the time of the crime he was on "automatic pilot," he will usually he acquitted.

         A) Distinguish
            1) The insanity defense will almost always lead to incarceration in a mental institution and an automatism defense will not.
            2) An automatism defense usually requires less evidence.

         B) Unconscious Act or Habit
            Habit is a bodily movement that otherwise is not a product of the efforts or determination of the actor. It is a fall back defense to encompass more liberal philosophies.

   c.   Forms of impaired consciousness:

       i.   Concussion: temporary brain damage due to physical trauma sometime produces a black-out during which a person may engage in previously learned behavior without full awareness thereof.

      ii.   Somnambulism: Night terrors are characterized by extreme fear & panic, intense vocalization and frenzied motor activity.

     iii.   Hypoglycemia: Because blood sugar is the exclusive source of energy for brain metabolism, hypoglycemia can lead to impaired functioning of the central nervous system.

   d.   The effect of finding "no voluntary act" is an outright acquittal.

   e.   Content and Function of the Voluntary Act
             Requirement:

       i.   The commission of a voluntary act is a necessary though insufficient condition of criminal liability. Holding an act involuntary precludes any criminal liability for that act.

      ii.   The distinction between voluntary and involuntary acts is a judgment call rather than a matter of definition. It is a normative issue.

E. Omissions as an Act

An omission is a failure to act.

1.   Distinguished from an Affirmative Act

EXAMPLE: Al watches Fonzie drown, there is no liability. Al pushes Fonzie into the water and Fonzie drowns, then Al is culpable. Because of Al's affirmative act of pushing Fonzie, then he had an affirmative duty to act to save Fonzie.

---

2. Legal Duty to Act
   For an omission to constitute a crime the defendant must first have a legal duty to act. MPC §2.01(3).

   a. Statute
      A law may categorically impose a duty to take positive action in certain situations.

   b. Relationship of Defendant to Victim Important
      Special relationship between defendant and victim
      i. Husband and wife or other blood relations.
      ii. Mere interdependence can fulfill this requirement also (ex: roommates).

   c. Contractual Duty
      A person may contract or hold a position where they must act. This could be a police officer, ambulance personnel or bodyguard. The state needs to demonstrate willfulness and knowledge of danger.

   d. Danger Caused by Defendant

Jones V. State, 900 S.W. 2d 392 (Tex. Ct. App. 1995)

Holding: The defendant was found to owe a duty to a 12-year-old girl that he had just raped who jumped from a bridge and drowned. The man was found guilty of rape and manslaughter.

   e. Assumes Responsibility
      One who voluntarily assumed the care of another or undertook to render aid to another assumes responsibility. This is particularly true if defendant leaves the victim worse off than before or dissuades other rescuers from helping victim since they see she has already started.

3. Defenses: Need Knowledge
   Knowledge is almost always required for conviction.
   a. If the defendant can demonstrate he was not cognizant of the facts that surrounded the duty to act then he may not be convicted

      b.   Statutory Duty to Know Underlying Facts
          Sometimes the person may be under a duty to *know* the underlying facts.
      c.   Strict Liability
          Sometimes, though rarely, the court may impose *strict liability* in knowing the facts that give rise to a duty.
      d.   Ignorance
          Ignorance that the law *imparts a legal duty* will not generally constitute a defense.

4.   Cases.

      a.   Crime by Omission.

Commonwealth v. Konz, 402 A.2d 692 (Pa.1979)

Facts: Mr. Konz, the deceased, decided to go off his insulin medication and to be healed by prayer. He promised, however, that if it became necessary, he would resume taking his insulin. When the deceased experienced an acute need for insulin, the defendants (his wife and his friend) did not give him insulin when he could no longer take it on his own.

Issue: Is Mrs. Konz guilty of involuntary manslaughter by failing to give aid to her husband?

Holding: Yes. Both defendants convicted. Mrs. Konz did have a duty to act through marriage to her husband. Mr. Erikson is being held liable on aiding and abetting an omission.

      b.   Failure to Summon Medical Aid.

People v. Robbins, 443 N.Y.S. 2d 1016 (App. Div. 1981)
It would be an unwarranted extension of the spousal duty of care to impose criminal liability for failure to summon medical aid for a competent adult spouse who has made a rational decision to eschew medical assistance.

c.   Unrelated Woman in House.

People v. Beardsley, 113 N.W. 1128 (Mich. 1907)
The fact that this woman was in his house created no such legal duty as exists in law and is due from a husband towards his wife. Mere moral obligation does not create a legal duty.

d.   Transporting from a public place to home.

People v. Oliver, 258 Cal. Rptr. 138 (Cal Ct. App. 1989)
Defendant drove the deceased, who was extremely drunk, to her home from a bar. By taking him from a public place, where others might have taken care to prevent him from injuring himself, to a private place -- her home -- where she alone can provide such care, she took charge of a person unable to prevent harm to himself. She owed the deceased a duty to prevent that risk from occurring by summoning aid.

e.   Legal Duty to Care for Children.

Jones v. United States, 308 F.2d 307 (D.C. Cir. 1962)
Defendant let two children starve in her basement. The trial court convicted her of involuntary manslaughter, but the appeals court reversed because the trial court never required the jury to find that defendant had a legal duty to care for the children.

f.   Omission to Perform a Legal Duty.

Barber v. Superior Court of Los Angeles County, 195 Cal. Rptr. 484 (Cal. Ct. App. 1983)

Facts: D, a doctor, convinced deceased's family that deceased had a very poor chance of recovery and the family agreed to take off all machines sustaining life. The deceased continued to breathe, however, without the respirator machine. D, after consultation with the family, then had the hydration and nourishment machines shut off, and the deceased died.

Issue: Should the defendants be held guilty of murder? What are the duties owed by a physician to a patient who has been reliably diagnosed as in a comatose state from which any meaningful recovery of cognitive brain function is exceedingly unlikely?

Holding: No. Defendant's omission to continue treatment, though intentional and with the knowledge that the patient would die, was not an unlawful failure to perform a legal duty.

V. CAUSATION

A. Facts of Causation

Must be "but for" the fact. If the result would have occurred anyway, then there is no causation.

1. Expansive Nature of Test
    This test is very liberal.
2. Substantial Factor Test
    This is where the 'but for" test does not exactly fit. The defendant's actions substantially contribute to the cause, it would not have likely been caused by itself but in conjunction with another it did.

B. Proximate Cause

1. Prosecution Must Prove
    Once it is determined that the defendant's actions caused the harm, the prosecution must prove beyond a reasonable doubt that the harm resulted is in close nexus with the act.
2. MPC § 2.03(2)(b)
    This is where the result involves the "same kind of injury" or harm that was intended by the defendant. The harm is the proximate cause of the act if it is not "too remote or incidental in its occurrence to have a just bearing on the actor's liability or on the gravity of his offense."

C. Unintended Victims

1. Transferred Intent Generally
    The fact that a victim is unintended does not prevent the actions of the injurer from being the proximate cause of the harm. Courts use the theory of transferred intent wherein an intent to injure one person will automatically be transferred to any unintended or unknown victim.

      a.   MPC § 2.03(2)(a)
      b.   Applies to Attempt

2.   Mistake of Identity
    This is not a defense.

For example, Howard Stern intends to kill Imus. He sees a person matching Imus's description enter the radio station. Howard shoots his .38 caliber handgun, jumps into his limo and speeds away. Later, Howard finds out he really shot the Greaseman. Howard is still guilty of First Degree Murder.

---

3.   Crimes of Recklessness or Negligence
    There usually needs to be a greater link of causation when dealing with recklessness and negligence when an unintended victim is injured.

      a.   Recklessness
          A defendant will probably not be guilty for any injury to the victim unless there is a significant risk of foreseeable harm to the defendant's position.
      b.   Negligence
          For the Defendant to be held guilty for negligent criminal acts, the victim would probably have to be in the foreseeable zone of danger.
      c.   MPC § 2.03(3)(a)
          The MPC states a defendant cannot escape guilty conduct merely because the victim was not within the foreseeable zone of danger. However, a person cannot be guilty of acts when the victim is too remote or accidental in its occurrence. For example, a person sees a group of people standing a mile away. He throws a rock at them. A huge wind grabs the rock and pushes it most of the way there, it comes down and skips across the water hitting a person in the eye. The rock thrower is not guilty of assault or battery.

D. Proximate Cause - Unintended Manner of Harm

1. Generally
   Courts are divided when an intended victim is harmed but in a manner not exactly intended.

   a. Not Guilty
      A person is not guilty when harm occurs from a bizarre or strange event. For example, Paula Cole was chasing Fiona Apple through a dance club to beat her up. While running away from Paula, a disco ball falls on Fiona seriously injuring her.

   b. MPC § 2.03(2)(b)
      A person is not guilty if the harm is "not within the purpose or the contemplation" of the defendant or if the harm is "too remote or accidental in its occurrence." For example, same fact situation as above except Paula Cole knows that the disco ball is going to fall any second. Paula purposely chases Fiona under the ball when it falls. Paula is guilty.

2. Unintended Harm but Foreseeable
   The defendant is guilty as long as there was no intervening cause resulting in the injury.

   a. A defendant takes the victims as they really are. For example, John Major has a rare blood condition only known to him. Gerry Adams purposefully hits John because he will not leave his homeland. John dies because a blood clot (related to his condition brought about by the injury) causes a heart attack. Gerry is guilty of murder.

   b. Attempted murder without an intervening cause that results in injuries also counts as attempted murder.

3. Intervening Acts

   a. Dependent Intervening Acts
      Defendant is not guilty. The event must be superseding. For example, Al Gore and James Buchanan fight. Al has to go to the hospital for a broken nose. En route to the hospital, the ambulance is hit by Ted who is drinking and driving. The result is that Al dies. James is not guilty of murder because Ted's guilty actions superseded James' action in the death of Al.

   b. Independent Intervening Act
      Defendant is usually not guilty. A person is not guilty as long as the action was unforeseeable.

4. Third Party Intervening Acts

   a. An act is generally intervening if:

      i. It was independent and unforeseeable; or
      ii. It was dependent on the defendant's act but abnormal. For example, Jack was hit by Diane's car and she drives away. While waiting for an ambulance John robs Jack in his helpless state. Diane is not guilty of robbery.

   b. Medical Malpractice After Act
      This is never a superseding cause unless it is so grossly unusual. For example, Deb slaps Brian. Brian goes to the hospital. The hospital decides to give Brian a shot. The hospital accidentally gives Brian a lethal dose of penicillin. Deb is not guilty of murder. In the alternative, Pete runs a red light and crashes into Peggy's car. Peggy suffers severe head trauma. Once in the hospital the doctors make a mistake in brain surgery and Peggy dies. Pete is guilty of manslaughter.

5. Victim's Actions as Superseding
   The victim's own actions may act as a superseding cause. The test is foreseeability of the victim's act by the defendant. The victim's actions must be grossly abnormal for conduct not to be chargeable.

   a. Suicide
      Suicide is not a superseding event unless there is evidence that a suicide plan was planned prior to the defendant's conduct. For example, Luke rapes Laura. Laura, unable to deal with the crime perpetrated on her, commits suicide. Luke is guilty of murder.

   b. MPC § 210.5(1). The defendant is criminally liable if the action "purposely causes such suicide by force, duress, or deception."

   c. Refusal of Medical Aid. Refusing medical aid is never a superseding cause.

   d. Injury During Escape. Almost never a superseding cause unless the action of the victim is grossly abnormal and bizarre.

6. Other than Human. These acts are intervening superseding events:

   a. Acts of God;

   b. Attack of animals that are not under the control of the defendant and are not known to the defendant.

VI.   CRIMES AGAINST THE PERSON: HOMICIDE

A.   Murder

1. Generally
    a. Murder vs. Manslaughter

        i.   Killing without malice.
             Malice aforethought differentiates manslaughter from murder.
        ii. Involuntary manslaughter.
             Involuntary manslaughter is the unlawful and unintentional killing of another person.
        iii. Voluntary manslaughter.
             A killing that could be a murder may be treated as voluntary manslaughter if there is the existence of a mitigating factor such as adequate provocation (e.g., heat of passion).

    b. <u>Definition</u>
        Murder is the killing of a human being by another with malice aforethought. Malice aforethought does not always mean premeditation. Premeditation is only a factor which may aggravate a homicide from second degree murder to first degree murder, once it has been established that the homicide was murder and not manslaughter.

        i.   Absent any enhancing factors, a killing with "malice aforethought" is second-degree murder.
        ii. Malice
             Malice is the intent to kill, lacking any mitigating factor.

2.   First degree: Aggravated Murder.

    a.   Malicious Murder

        i.   Express malice
            Express malice is an intentional, unmitigated killing. It is an intent to kill.

        ii.   Implied malice
            Implied malice encompassed three presumed moral equivalents of intent:

            A)   Intent to inflict serious bodily harm. This has been omitted from the MPC and most penal statutes.

            B)   Depraved heart or Extreme indifference to life.

                1)   Definition.   Extreme recklessness with respect to serious risk of harm to human life, or extreme indifference to human life, beyond the unintentional state of mind that might otherwise establish reckless involuntary manslaughter.

                2)   Effect.   It aggravates the charge of manslaughter to murder.

                3)   Felony Murder.
                    Felony murder is inadvertently killing another human being during the course of committing certain dangerous felonies.

        iii. MPC

            A)   Intent To Kill
                Criminal homicide is murder when it is committed purposely or knowingly; OR

            B)   Depraved Heart Murder:
                Depraved heart murder is recklessly committed under the circumstances manifesting extreme indifference to human life.

EXAMPLE: BillyJoe shoots his shotgun into a house where there is a group of people. He was not trying to kill anyone, but was just trying to scare them. JoeBob dies of the gun wound. BillyJoe is guilty of murder.

C) Felony Murder.

Such recklessness and indifference are presumed if the defendant is pursuing or is the accomplice in commission of or in an attempt to commit or flight from committing or attempting to commit one of the following serious felonious crimes: murder, assault, robbery, rape, deviant sexual intercourse by force or threat of force, arson, burglary, kidnapping, or felonious escape.

b. Premeditated Murder.

i. First degree murder needs premeditation or malice aforethought.

ii. Circumstantial evidence can result in a finding of premeditation.

iii. Time required for premeditation is as follows:

A) No substantial amount of time need elapse between formation of intent to kill and execution of murder. A moment is all that is necessary.

B) Some modern courts require reasonable time for premeditation.

iv. The following factors are to be considered:

A) To Prove Planning:

1) Having prior possession of the weapon and/or bring a weapon

2) Transporting the victim prior to death to another place.

3) Lying in wait (sneak attack)

4) Prior stalking or surveillance of the victim.

v. To Prove Motive:

A) Prior conduct of victim known to anger the defendant.

B) Death of victim known to benefit the killer.

vi. Nature of killing:

A) Interruption and subsequent renewal of the acts leading to the murder.

For example, Tyson and Holyfield get into a fight over a belt in the school yard. Tyson goes home and gets really upset. Later that evening, Tyson goes out and finds Holyfield's house. He knocks on the door and Holyfield answers. Tyson jumps and proceeds to bite off parts of Holyfield's body until he is dead. Tyson is guilty of murder.

B) The murder was such an exact and intricate preconceived design or plan.

For example, O.J. starts dating Nicole. Nicole's mother, fearing that something awful will happen to Nicole, plots the death of O.J. Mother decides to hire a hit man who will strike at O.J. while she and Nicole are at a party. Then, she hires another man to take and bury the body in Alaska. Nicole's mother is guilty of first-degree murder.

C) Intoxication

Intoxication can mitigate the circumstances because the ability to deliberate (or any *mens rea*) may be found to have been negated. First-degree murder statute states the killer must have "knowingly or purposely" killed. If the defendant can show that he was so intoxicated as not to form the specific intent of purposely or knowingly then he is not guilty.

3. Intent to Kill

    a. Intent Generally
Defendant either purposely wanted to kill the victim or knew that there is a substantial certainty of death. Intent can be proven by circumstantial evidence. In most states intent to kill (murder) is divided into two categories:

        i. First Degree: Murders committed with deliberation and premeditation; and

        ii. Second degree: All other types of murders.

    b. *State v. Jean Harris*, 722 S.W. 2d 436 (Tex Ct. App. 1986)
Holding: The defendant was convicted of second-degree murder, intentional killing without premeditation after killing the doctor with whom she had an affair. The court held that she was too upset to premeditate the murder, but not too upset to have the intent to kill. Defendant chose to use the accidental killing defense instead of the manslaughter defense.

        i. Both objective and subjective provocation were adequate;

        ii. A reasonable person may have cooled off but the Defendant could have argued that finding another woman's lingerie was the last cumulative factor.

4. Intent to Cause Serious Bodily Harm

    a. MPC
Intent to cause serious bodily harm is not recognized in the MPC.

    b. No Intent
Even if the defendant did not intend to kill but only to do serious bodily harm, he can be found guilty of murder. Knowledge that injury is highly likely is sufficient to find murder.

    c. Subjective Knowledge
Generally, this knowledge is subjective not objective.

5.   Depraved Heart Murder

    a.   Recklessness
       The defendant is guilty of murder if he acted recklessly under the circumstances manifesting extreme indifference to the value of human life. If the defendant acted recklessly without manifesting extreme indifference to the value of human life it would have been manslaughter.

    b.   Felony murder presumptions
       Such recklessness and indifference are presumed in felony murder if:

         i.   Depraved-Heart Murder
            The actor is a principal or an accomplice in committing, attempting or fleeing after committing felony murder.

            A) Gross
                Substantial and unjustifiable homicidal risk of which the actor *should have been aware (objective standard)*.
            B) Ordinary Recklessness
                Substantial and unjustifiable homicidal risk of which the actor *was aware and consciously disregarded.*
            C) Gross Recklessness
                Very substantial and unjustifiable homicidal risk of which the actor *was aware and consciously disregarded,* e.g., depraved heart murder.

        ii. *Is the risk justifiable?*
            This is a cost/benefit analysis of justifiable risk.
        iii. *Did the actor realize the risk?*
            MPC states that one needs a conscious disregard of the risk for any form of recklessness.

B.   Felony Murder

1. First Degree Felony Murder
    First-degree felony murder occurs during the commission or attempted commission of the following felonies: burglary, rape, robbery, arson, kidnapping, felonious escape, and deviant sexual intercourse by threat or force.

2. Second Degree
    Second degree felony murder is killing that occurs during the commission or attempted commission of some other dangerous felonies not enumerated in the specific state's statute.

3. Common law
    The common law definition of felony murder is very liberal. If a person killed someone while committing any felony they were strictly liable.

4. MPC
    The MPC rejects the felony murder rule because the defendant can be convicted under extreme reckless murder or intent to kill murder. The rationale for this is that there is no need to hold an accidental death to murder.

    a. Presumption
        The MPC establishes a rebuttable presumption of recklessness manifesting an extreme indifference to human life where the defendant is a principal or accomplice in the commission of one of the enumerated felonies.

    b. Jury Question
        If an unintentional killing occurs during the commission of a felony, the prosecution (state) is presumably entitled to go to the jury in the issue of extreme indifference to human life.

5. Notes on Felony Murder.

    a. Dangerous to Life Felonies.
        Felony murder is dangerous to felonies which, but for felony murder, would be punishable by life in prison.

    b. Proximate Cause.
        The commission of the felony must be the proximate cause of the murder. For example, a man botches a robbery attempt at a bank and takes everyone hostage including the bank owner's husband. At home the bank owner turns on the television, sees the situation and has a heart attack and dies. The defendant is not guilty of felony murder. (*See infra*, Section G.1.c. for similar situation with opposite result).

    c. Narrowing the Scope.
        The scope of definition of the element of "in the commission or the attempted commission" is construed in a narrow definition.

    d. No Merger
        The underlying felony should be independent of the homicide and not merge with it.

6. Application of Felony Murder

    a. Felonies that are inherently dangerous to human life:
        i. Majority View
            The dangerousness of the felony is judged in the abstract. That is, is the felony dangerous in and of itself? For example, murder, rape, robbery and arson are inherently dangerous.
        ii. Minority View
            The dangerousness of the felony is determined by applying it to the facts of the case. This takes a more liberal reading of felony murder because a death may occur even though a less dangerous felony has been committed.

iii. Thin-Skull Rule

People v. Stamp, 82 Cal. Rptr. 598 (Cal. Ct. App. 1970)

Holding: The court held that where the victim died from a heart-attack shortly after the defendant robbed his store, defendant was guilty of felony murder. The court applied the "thin skull" rule and held that the defendant "takes his victim as he finds him." Proximate cause is found even though the death was not foreseeable because the thin skull rule holds that where injury, no matter how slight, occurs, and this causes greater injury, the defendant is liable for all injuries, foreseeable or not.

2. Commission of a Crime
   Felony murder must occur "in the commission of" a felony.
   a. A coincidence is not enough.
   b. Escaping after the commission of an offense is still considered.
      i. An immediate flight from commission is still considered in the commission.
      ii. If officers are in hot pursuit it is still in the commission. That is, if the bank robbers jump in their car and drive away. Ten minutes later they run a red light in their hopes of making a clean get-away and kill a pedestrian crossing the street.
      iii. If the felons still have the stolen goods on them it is in the commission.

3. Felony must be independent of the killing

   a. Merger Doctrine
      If the facts underlying the offense committed are the same as the facts needed for felony murder, they merge into the lesser included offense and preclude application of the felony murder doctrine.
      i. Aggravated assault would probably merge because the same underlying facts of the felony produced the murder. That is, it was intentional attack.
      ii. Robbery would not merge. There are separate underlying facts composing robbery and murder

State v. Lucas, 759 P.2d 90 (Kan. 1988)

Facts: A child died after being abused, beaten and left unconscious in the bathtub.

Holding: There is no felony murder application because actions of child abuse and the homicide merge so that there is one action for the death.

4   Accomplice Liability

Accomplice liability for all co-felons occurs if the killing is committed by one of them while in the furtherance of the felony.

  a.   Rebuttable

If the other felons can show that the murder was not done in the furtherance of the robbery, but rather as a revenge killing by the principal killer, they may escape liability.

  b.   Fellow Co-Felon

States are split as to whether the death of a co-felon is grounds for felony murder.

For example, Bonnie and Clyde rob a bank. The police catch up to them at an old abandoned Cape Cod house. A shoot out ensues. During the shoot out Bonnie is killed by the police. Can Clyde be charged with felony murder because the police killed Bonnie?

In some states, the death of a co-felon is not a basis for felony murder (e.g., N.Y.). In other states (e.g., N.J.), if death of a co-felon occurs by anyone, the felony murder rule applies.

3.   Second Degree Murder

  a.   First Degree vs. Second Degree

The difference between first and second-degree murder is that the killer did not form the requisite premeditation or did not make any prior planning before the murder.

  b.   Seriousness

Where there is intent to cause serious injury and the person dies, the charge is second-degree murder.

EXAMPLE: Jack sees a photographer snapping his picture. Jack grabs a baseball bat and swings to hit the cameraman. Jack hits the camera and the man and knocks them to the ground. The man breaks his neck when he falls.

---

      c.   Indifference to Life
         A person is guilty of second-degree murder if his/her actions are in complete disregard of human life. For example, Don believes it is fun to stand on the top of his 6-story building and drop lead balls off the top. He does this not to hit the people but to see how close he can get without hitting them. One day Don miscalculates and hits Bob in the head, killing him instantly.

      d.   MPC.
         MPC does not distinguish between first and second-degree murder. However, almost all the states keep the distinction on the books.

C. Manslaughter.

    1.   In General.
       a.   MPC Intent:
           i.   For Murder
              The mens rea is purpose or knowledge.
           ii. For Manslaughter
              The mens rea is recklessness.
           iii. For Negligent Homicide
              The mens rea is negligence.
       b.   Manslaughter Defined
         Manslaughter is the conscious disregard of a perceived homicidal risk or substantial risk of death.
       c.   MPC
           i.   MPC does not distinguish between voluntary and involuntary manslaughter. It is merely manslaughter.
           ii. Intent is recklessness

       d.   Voluntary vs. Involuntary Manslaughter

           i.   Voluntary manslaughter is:
              A) Killing done intentionally with knowledge.
              B) A first-degree crime.

    ii. Involuntary manslaughter is:
- A) Killing another out of ordinary negligence, gross negligence, reckless conduct; or
- B) Committed during the intentional commission of another crime, not a felony.
- C) Almost always a second-degree crime.

2. Voluntary Manslaughter
Vehicular manslaughter is defined as the intentional killing. That is, with purpose or knowledge, of another human being as a product of provocation or heat of passion. This crime carries greater penalties than involuntary manslaughter.

   a. MPC
     i. The MPC does not distinguish between voluntary and involuntary manslaughter.
     ii. Mental state is recklessness, OR
     iii. Killing is done with purpose or knowledge where the actor is under extreme emotional disturbance under which there is a *reasonable excuse.*

For example, husband who just got fired comes home early and finds wife in bed with best friend. Husband pulls out gun and kills wife.

---

iv.   Therefore, if the excuse is reasonable, murder could be reduced to voluntary manslaughter or voluntary manslaughter can be reduced to involuntary manslaughter. A successful defense does not get the defendant an acquittal, only a reduction in the charge and penalty.

   b. Adequacy of Provocation

     i. The MPC definition of *reasonable* is subjective. "Reasonableness" is determined from the viewpoint of a reasonable person in the perpetrator's situation under the circumstances as he believes them to be.
     ii. There is a two-part Test of Reasonableness
- A) Adequacy of provocation (Objective);
- B) Is the person really upset (Subjective).

     iii. Four Requirements for the Defense of Heat of Passion

- A) Objective Standard for Provocation.

1) <u>Definition.</u> Defendant acts in response to provocation that would be sufficient to cause a reasonable man to lose his self control.

2) Common law adequacy of provocation:
   a) Some of the categories where the courts found adequate provocation were:
      i) The victim attacked first and the defendant used deadly force;
      ii) Mutual combat between victim and defendant;
      iii) Unlawful arrest of the defendant;
      iv) The defendant witnessed the victim committing adultery;
      v) A violent assault on a relation (e.g., daughter raped and defendant-father goes and kills rapist).
   b) The court examines factors that would make an ordinary reasonable man very angry to the point of losing his normal self-control.
   c) Not words. Words alone would not be sufficient provocation.
   d) Not revenge. Revenge on the victim does not constitute sufficient provocation.
   e) Fear would not suffice because it was not thought to make a man angry.

3) Adequacy of Provocation Today:
   a) In most jurisdictions, what is an objectively adequate provocation is determined on a reasonable basis. In these jurisdictions, there are no more categories where the courts would find sufficient provocation.
   b) Moreover, words alone are sufficient provocation.
   c) Also, the MPC states that the cumulative effects of fear over time may be sufficient provocation.

B) Subjective Standard for Provocation. Defendant does in fact act in the heat of passion. Actual provocation is a subjective determination of whether the actor was in an "excited heat of passion" when he committed the crime.

C) Objective Standard for Cooling Off Period. The lapse of time between the provocation and the killing is not great enough that a reasonable man would have "cooled off." Objective "cooling off" period is an objective examination of how long a reasonable man would take to "cool off."

   1) The modern view allows the "cumulative effect" of various factors such as fear to mitigate murder or voluntary manslaughter because it recognizes that a defendant may never really have been able to fully "cool off." Thus when he does kill, it may be that the "heat of passion" situation of pent up aggression caused him to take a life.

   2) The common law did not allow "cumulative effects" to mitigate murder because the contention was that there was adequate "cooling off" after each episode and a reasonable defendant would not stay in the heat of passion. This goes to the last provocative event.

iv. Subjective Standard of Cooling Off. Defendant in fact had not cooled off.

Freddo v. State, 155 S.W. 170 (Tenn. 1913).

Facts: Freddo was raised in an orphanage and then in foster care. He was morally well-trained, quiet and peaceable and respectful of women beyond the average young man of his age. Freddo worked with the deceased and several times asked that the deceased desist from using "Son of a bitch". The deceased was also warned by a mutual friend that his foul-mouth was particularly offensive to Freddo. One day at work, while the deceased was squatting down attending to a locomotive cylinder, oil was spilled on the deceased's toolbox. Deceased blamed Freddo and called him a "Son of a bitch". Freddo observed deceased rising and coming at Freddo with his hands behind his back. Fearing that he was about to be struck , and enraged by deceased's use of the epithet, Freddo hit deceased with a steel bar, killing him.

Issue: If Freddo killed deceased under the impulse of sudden passion, was his passionate resentment sufficient to reduce the grade of the crime from murder to voluntary manslaughter?

Holding: No. While the combination of the epithet and the deceased's act of rising make a cause of adequate provocation, the jury found that the deceased was not in a position to assault Freddo.

Reasoning: Passion is not sufficient to reduce the grade of the crime from murder to voluntary manslaughter unless the provocation is of such a character as would, in the mind of an average reasonable man, stir resentment likely to cause violence, obscure reason and lead the defendant to act from passion rather than judgment.

People v. Casassa, 404 N.E.2d 1310 (N.Y. 1998)

Facts: Decedent broke up with Defendant who became obsessed and, after essentially stalking her for three weeks, stabbed her to death with a steak knife.

Issue: Did Defendant establish the affirmative defense of "extreme emotional disturbance" to reduce crime from murder to manslaughter?

Holding: No. Defendant's reaction to events was not reasonable; it was peculiar to him. The "extreme emotional disturbance" is broader in scope than the "heat of passion" doctrine, and requires both a subjective and an objective analysis. According to the MPC, the first part of the analysis is subjective but the second part is objective.

    iv.   Provocation on Heat of Passion

        A) There are three elements of provocation:
            1) Heat of Passion. Defendant is in the heat of passion (Defendant is in fact provoked.)
            2) Provocation. The defendant was legally adequate provoked.
            3) Reasonable person standard. A reasonable person would be similarly enraged given the same circumstances.

B) All provocation murders are essentially second-degree murders without provocation.
   1) If victim provoked the defendant, then in a sense, the victim is a cause of his own death.
   2) People under these circumstances are not going to evaluate deterrent arguments.
   3) Lesser crime because a provoked killer is less dangerous than another killer.

C) Cooling Off Time - Three-step analysis of the question:
   1) Defendant's passion must not have abated.
   2) The passage of a period of time sufficient for reason to be restored will preclude the defense as a matter of law.
   3) It is in any event a question for the jury whether a reasonable person would have cooled off in the interval between the provocation and the act of killing.

D) Objective Standard
   1) Sufficiency of provocation and passage of time to cool down both are measured by an objective standard.
   2) The adequacy of provocation should not be judged by reference to the accused's special sensitivities. Deterrence is impossible if a completely subjective standard of conduct is applied -- as opposed to a purpose of punishment -- to measure moral blameworthiness and punish proportionately.

E) The relevance of mental abnormality
   1) Provocation. Mental abnormality is not relevant to whether provocation was reasonable if we maintain an objective standard.

        2) "Imperfect" justification. It is a defense to an intentional killing if it can be shown that the defendant believed it a necessary response to unlawful deadly force and that the response was reasonable under the circumstances. Usually courts will reduce the charge if only the subjective element were met. In these jurisdictions, mental abnormality should be relevant.

  b. Involuntary Manslaughter
    i. Defined
      Involuntary manslaughter is the unintentional killing resulting from reckless or negligent conduct or from the intentional commission of another crime, not a felony.
    ii. MPC §210.3
      A) Criminal Homicide
        Criminal homicide establishes manslaughter when it is committed recklessly.

      B) Sentence
        It is a felony in the second degree punishable by a minimum of one to three years and a maximum of 10 years in prison.
    iii. MPC § 210.4
      A) Criminal homicide constitutes negligent homicide when the act is committed negligently.

      B) Felony
        It is a felony in the third degree.
        <u>Sentence</u>. It is punishable by a minimum of one year in prison with a maximum of five years.
    iv. Negligent and Reckless Homicide:

      A) Gross Negligence by Omission of Duty to Act

State v. O'Brien, 46 N.W. 752 (Iowa 1967).

Holding: The court asserted a person could be guilty of manslaughter by an omission to act (gross negligence) if he had a duty to act and then breached the duty which breach then caused the death.

1) <u>Minority Rule</u>
   In a minority of jurisdictions, ordinary negligence will support manslaughter.

2) <u>Majority Rule</u>
   In most states a gross negligence standard will support a finding of manslaughter. In almost all jurisdictions, a finding of recklessness will support a manslaughter conviction.

B) Recklessness by Omission of Affirmative Duty to Act.

Commonwealth v. Welansky, 55 N.E. 2d 902 (Mass. 1944)

Holding: The court considered that disregard of others was sufficient for the sort of recklessness, which may support manslaughter. The nightclub owner did not provide safe fire exits and patrons died during a fire. Usually there must be an affirmative act but when one is charged with the safety of others and consciously does an unsafe thing, inaction may suffice. The standard here was willfully, wantonly, and recklessly. Willfully indicates an affirmative act, not culpability. The affirmative act was not providing fire exits. Recklessly was the culpability. The court articulated that grave danger to others must have been apparent and the defendant must have chosen to run the risk rather than alter his conduct so as to avoid the act or omission, which caused the harm. The difference is the degree of risk and the voluntary taking of that risk.

C) Negligence: Reasonable Person Standard.

State v. Williams, 484 P.2d 1167 (Wash. Ct. App. 1971)

Facts: Defendants were negligent in failing to take an infant to the doctor. As a result, the baby dies.

Issue: Does simple negligence satisfy the *mens rea* element of involuntary manslaughter?

Holding: Yes. Ordinary caution is the kind of caution that a man of reasonable prudence would exercise under the same or similar conditions. In this case, a reasonably prudent person would have sought medical attention before the defendants did. They knew such care was available having used it before.

NOTE: Under the MPC, the Defendants would not be convicted of manslaughter because they were not reckless (§210.3). MPC has a gross negligence standard that takes into account the gravity of harm, likelihood of harm and other surrounding factors.

---

  c. Misdemeanor Manslaughter
    i. Defined
        Misdemeanor manslaughter is defined as the occurrence of an unlawful act which results in unintentional death of another human being, e.g., vehicular homicide. To be convicted on misdemeanor manslaughter, you need the *mens rea* of the underlying crime.
        • Liability: The nature of the act ascertains the liability. If it is *mala in se, then* it is strict liability. If it is *mala prohibita, then* the prosecutor needs to show causation.
    ii. MPC
        A) The MPC has no misdemeanor manslaughter for the following reasons:
          1) Misdemeanor manslaughter is already covered under negligent homicide.
          2) The MPC is averse to strict liability because a person should not be convicted of a crime without the necessary *mens rea*.

B) The lowest level of homicide under the MPC is negligent homicide. Thus, the MPC will never hold a defendant strictly liable for manslaughter. There must be a showing of at least negligence.

iii. Three Part Test for misdemeanor manslaughter

A) Determine the offense. Is defendant guilty of a misdemeanor?

B) Determine whether the offense is *mala in se* or *mala prohibita*?

C) If the offense is *mala in se,* then the defendant is strictly liable and he is guilty of misdemeanor manslaughter.

If the offense, *mala prohibita* then causation has to be determined.

iv. *Mala in se vs. Mala Prohibita*:

A) *Mala in Se*
   1) Definition.   Crimes that are bad in themselves, e.g., robbery, arson, rape, are *mala in se.*
   2) Liability
      If a *mala in se* crime is committed and death results, you will be held strictly liable for the death.

B) *Mala Prohibita*
   1) Definition. Crimes that are bad because the legislature says so are mala prohibita.
   2) For example, speeding, driving without a license, sale of intoxicating liquors to minors are mala prohibita. *Test; See infra.*

v.   Three-Prong Test for *Mala Prohibita*. The following
tests must be met to meet the standards of mala
prohibita:

A) A necessary and actual consequence of the
misdemeanor; or

B) Proximate result of the act; or

C) An unlawful excess, e.g. excess speed, which
caused the resulting death.
Unlawful excess theory states that if an unlawful
excess (usually in speed of an automobile)
caused the death, the defendant is guilty. If
however, the defendant can show that the victim
would have died regardless of the excess in
speed, he may be exonerated.

vi. Vehicular Homicide

A) There are two types:
1) Vehicular homicide has the following
characteristics:
a) Requires a material deviation from the
basic standard of care or ordinary
negligence; and
b) Carries a sentence of less than one year
in prison plus fine.
2) Aggravated Vehicular Homicide:
Felonious behavior such as reckless driving,
DUI, DWI, or evading the police is
considered aggravated vehicular homicide.

B) MPC
The MPC makes no distinction between
negligent homicide and vehicular homicide. To
be found guilty of a misdemeanor, the
prosecution need only show negligence or
recklessness.

VII. CRIMES AGAINST THE PERSON: LESS THAN HOMICIDE

A. Rape

1. Definition
    Rape is sexual intercourse by a man with a person, other than his wife, without consent.
    a. Most states have removed the common law requirement of "other than his wife" so that a man can be convicted of raping his wife.
    b. In a minority of states, only a man can be convicted of rape. A woman, by definition, cannot rape a man. The majority of states define rape in gender neutral terms now.
2. Vaginal
    In a minority of states, rape consists only of vaginal sex, not oral or anal sex. These other acts are considered under the separate crime of deviate sexual intercourse. The majority of states and the MPC include oral and anal intercourse in the definition of rape.
3. Without Consent
    a. Force
        Intercourse by force would be without consent. However, if the victim consents during the rape then it is no longer rape, unless the victim's sole reason for the consent is to avoid injury.
    b. Threats
        Intercourse by threats of injury or force is without consent. States differ as to whether threat of revelation of secrets constitutes lack of consent.

    c. Fraud
        Intercourse by fraud is usually considered rape. For example, if a woman goes to a gynecologist for an examination and she approves the placement of instruments into her vagina and while under drugs he has sex with her, this is fraud.

i. Minority
A minority of states would not hold this as a rape.

ii. Wrong person
If a man and a woman get drunk together and he convinces her he is Don Juan (her fantasy man) and has sex with her under consent (thinking he is Don Juan) some courts are split as to whether this is rape.

d. Incapacity to Consent
Intercourse when the victim is incapacitated, hence incapable of consent, is usually considered rape.
For example, if Veronica gets so drunk that she passes out and Archie has sexual intercourse with her, this is rape. However, in some states it depends on past circumstances. Change the fact pattern so that for the past 20 years, every time Veronica drinks, she passes out and Archie has sex with her. Veronica knows they have sex after the fact every time. This may not be rape because there is an implied pattern of consent.

4. Mens Rea
Most jurisdictions require only lack of victim's consent. At least one jurisdiction allows a jury instruction where "substantial evidence of equivocal conduct that would have led a defendant to reasonably and in good faith believe consent existed where it did not."

5. Statutory Rape
Sex with a girl under a certain age, regardless of consent, is statutory rape:
a. Statutory rape is a strict liability crime.
b. It is no defense that the girl reasonably looked to be of age.
c. It is no defense that the girl lied about her age, unless it was part of a greater scheme of entrapment.

B. Robbery

1. Definition

    Robbery is the theft of personal property of another, from the other's person or presence, by force or threat of force or in conjunction with another felony of the first or second degree, with the intent to deprive the victim of his possession permanently.

    a. Must prove all of the elements of larceny, *infra*; plus

    b. Taken from the victim's person or presence; and must be taken from the victim and the victim must generally know that the object is being taken. This need not be taken off the person but an object within the presence of the victim. For example, James Dean is leaning on his car. A carjacker comes up with a knife and tells James to step away from the car. James complies and the carjacker steals the car. This would be robbery (most states have defined car theft as grand theft auto). See MPC § 222.1.

    c. By force or intimidation.

        i. Force;
        ii. Use of drugs or intoxication;
        iii. Threats of force against victim, victim's family or friends or anyone else present at the crime scene. However, that threat must be of an immediate serious bodily injury, not some future injury;
        iv. Not pickpocket because the person is not aware of the theft.

2. Concurrence of Actus Reus and Mens Rea
    The perpetrator must intend to steal prior to or during the commission of the robbery by force or intimidation, within the same incident. Circumstances may elevate an intended simple larceny into a robbery.

C. Assault

1. Definition

   Assault is the attempted or actual causation of bodily injury to another knowingly, purposefully, or recklessly, or negligent causation of bodily injury to another with a deadly weapon, or the attempt by physical menace to put another in fear of imminent serious bodily injury.

2. Mens Rea

   An attempt to frighten is not enough. Something more must be shown, that a battery would have otherwise occurred, that is:

   a. Assault includes attempted battery. One may possess the mental state to commit the battery (intent to commit a battery).

   b. Willful and probable.

3. Actus Reus

   The perpetrator must have proximity to the actual completion of the crime. Most modern statutes define an assault as having the ability to succeed (factual possibility).
   Conditional Assault: A person is guilty of assault for example, even if he refrains from hurting the victim by demanding the victim's purse as a condition for not hurting the victim.

4. Fear of Battery

   A majority of states also prosecute for placing another in fear of a battery. See conditional assault *supra*.
   a. Intent to cause fear;
   b. Victim must be in fear and be aware of the assault.

> For example, Sylvester attempts to push a piano off a ten-story building onto Tweety. Tweety does not know the danger as he walks by. Sylvester is not guilty of assault because Tweety is unaware of the harm.

      c.   Fearful conduct. The perpetrator must instill fear that a reasonable person would understand as cause for fear or harm to her person. For instance, Whitman stands on the Jersey side of a bridge and threatens to hit Pataki on the nose, who is standing on the New York side of the bridge. There is no assault because there is no reasonable cause for fear or harm.

D. Battery

1.   Definition
Battery is the unlawful application of force to another person that results in harm or an offensive touching of another person.

2.   Actus Reus

      a.   No Injury
No injury is required for the crime of battery to occur. For example, Clinton grabs the breast of an intern who did not want to be grabbed. Clinton is guilty of sexual battery.

      b.   Indirect touching
The perpetrator need not be the object that does the touching. For example, a perpetrator uses an umbrella to poke the victim or to push over a plant that hits the victim.

      c.   Modern State Statutes
Most modern statutes require that a physical or mental harm occur to the victim before prosecution.

3. Mens Rea

   a. Negligence
   Most modern statutes allow for criminal negligence to be the mental state for prosecution.

   b. Consent
   Consent is a defense to battery. If a person consented to being touched then there is no crime, unless the perpetrator goes beyond the consent. For example, a patient authorizes a dentist to fix some cavities. The patient is drugged and the dentist subsequently decides to pull two teeth. The dentist has committed battery because the patient only consented to the fixing, but not pulling, of teeth.

4. Degrees of Battery
Battery can either be a misdemeanor (simple battery) or a felony (aggravated battery).

E. False Imprisonment

1. Definition
False imprisonment is the unlawful confinement or restraint of another human being within an area.

2. Actus Reus
The defendant must knowingly confine a person to an area either by force or threats.

   a. Blocking Insufficient.
   Just because a person blocks one direction does not imply false imprisonment has occurred, so long as other directions of movement are possible.

   b. Area
   It does not have to be a physically confining area. A person could be imprisoned in the middle of a football field, as long as no reasonable means of escape are possible.

3. Mens Rea
The defendant must have intended to confine the victim.

4. Unlawful
   The detainment must have been without authority. Police and other law enforcement officials have a right (limited in scope and time) to detain. Others, such as security personnel and others involved with safety have a more limited right to detain as well.

F. Kidnapping

1. Definition
   Kidnapping is the unlawful capture of a person and a movement of the person to another area.

2. Actus reus
   a. By force
   b. By threats
   c. Fraud
   d. The victim must be aware of and not consent to the kidnapping.
      However, in some instances, a person could subsequently discover they had been kidnapped for a time.

3. Mens Rea
   The perpetrator must have intended to confine or move the intended victim.

VIII. CRIMES AGAINST PROPERTY

A. Burglary

1. Definition
    Burglary is the breaking and entering into the dwelling house of another in the nighttime with the intent to commit a felony inside. Some states include a daytime act as well, reducing the crime to a felony of the third, rather than second, degree.

    a. Breaking and entering could be by actual or constructive trespass into the dwelling:
        i.   Actual trespass means physically breaking the door or window, using picks to open a locked door, or just opening a shut door.
        ii. Constructive trespass includes fraud (act as a repairman to gain entry), threat of force, through an open window, or a third party co-conspirator who is authorized allows entry to one who is not authorized.
    b. A dwelling is the house of another and includes curtilage to the house (ex: garage, barn). It must be another person's dwelling house, not a boat, not a warehouse, not a car.
    c. Nighttime is the common sense definition of nighttime and is based on sunlight.
    d. Intent to commit a felony.
        At time of entry, the person must have intended to commit a felony (murder, rape, arson, robbery, etc.). If the person broke in only wanting a place to sleep for an evening, then there is no burglary but mere trespass, a misdemeanor.

2. Entry

    a. By the body;

    b. By an instrument.

    For example, a person is in a tree outside a house with poison on a stick. The person pushes open the window and inserts the poison stick over the sleeping man. This is an entry and will be considered burglary with intent.

3. Modern

Most states have eliminated the elements of a dwelling and nighttime so that entry into any structure at any time for the purposes of committing a felony is a burglary.

B.   Arson

1. Definition

Arson is the malicious burning of another's house.

2. Elements

The elements of arson are as follows:

    a. Malicious intent;

    b. Burning;

    Burning must be by some sort of fire. Acid is not enough unless fire results. Note however that the dwelling need not be damaged nor destroyed.

    i. A fire that is quickly extinguished is still arson.

    ii. Not acid.

    iii. Not smoke damage.

    iv. Not explosions unless a fire results.

    c. Another's house;

    A person cannot commit arson upon his own house (house burning). It is based on either possession (tenant, roommate) or ownership. Traditionally, the only type of structure that can be a target of arson was a dwelling, not a warehouse or business.

3. Mens Rea

Arson intent is malice. Malice exists when the perpetrator intends to burn the dwelling. Negligence is insufficient.

4. Modern Trend
   a. Most states have eliminated the limitation that the property be a dwelling and most simply require that it be a structure.
   b. Most states include explosions and cover personal property not just real property.

C.   Larceny

1. Definition
   Larceny is a trespassory taking and carrying away of another's personal property with the intent to deprive the owner of possession.
   a. Trespassory
      i.   Without the owners consent;
      ii. Larceny by Deception
           This is where the victim's permission is obtained by deception, (e.g., a sidewalk card game scam.) Requires misrepresentation or deception to gain possession or ownership.
   b. Taking;
      The person exercises dominion and control over the object such that it would delineate possession.
      i.   Committed personally; or,
      ii. Having another person get the object.
   c. Carrying away.
      The slightest movement with intent will suffice.

      i.   Examples.

EXAMPLE 1: A person decides to steal a watch. They touch it with the intent to take, and move it 1mm. That will suffice for larceny.

EXAMPLE 2: A person picks up a watch to see if ID is on it and finds none. The person puts the watch down. The person then decides to steal it but is apprehended. There is no larceny.

---

      ii. Modern Trend.
           Most states have eliminated the need to carry away and use "exercise of control" instead.

77

d. Another's.

From another's superior interest in possession or ownership. There is no larceny if the defendant was already in lawful possession, custody or ownership. In the latter case, it would be considered embezzlement.

   i.   One cannot commit larceny against one's spouse.
   ii. Subject to exceptions, lost or mislaid objects may give rise to larceny if the defendant knows or should have known the owner.

e. Personal Property.

   i.   Larceny concerns only personal property not real property but also includes:
        A) Animals and other pets;
        B) Illegally owned objects (drugs, guns).
        C) Documents (Modern trend).
   ii. Fixtures are not included unless they are severed from the real property. Fixtures include:
        A) Crops
        B) Minerals
        C) House attachments.

f. The intent is to deprive the owner of possession of the property.

2. Modern Statutes
States usually prosecute for unlawful control or obtaining possession through unkept promises.

3. Mens Rea
The intent to permanently deprive the owner of possession or ownership of her property. If the defendant took the object with intent to pay for the object or return the object within a reasonable time then there is no intent to permanently deprive.

D. False Pretenses

1. Definition
   False Pretenses is the obtaining of title to property by means of a material false representation with the intent to defraud the owner.
   a. Obtaining title.
      A mere transfer of possession is not enough. One needs to transfer title of ownership to be accused of larceny.

   b. Property.
      i. Real property; or
      ii. Personal property.

   c. Material false representation elements are:
      i. Any fact past, present or future.
      ii. Material
         The representation must be of the concern and controlling factor in the decision of the owner parting with ownership of the property.
      iii. Causation
         The misrepresentation must have actually induced the transfer. The owner must have relied on the misrepresentation.

   d. Intent to defraud.
      The defendant must have knowingly made the false representation.

      i. No false pretense exists if the defendant believed what he said even if the belief were unreasonable.
      ii. Not knowing whether the statement was true is insufficient to establish lack of intent, without more, for purposes of acquittal.
      iii. Reckless disregard of the truth.

2. Larceny by Deception Distinguished
   In larceny by deception, the defrauder gets only possession of the item, not title.

3. Corroboration of Evidence
   Most states require something more than the victim's testimony to convict. This is to protect legitimate buyers from sellers who later change their minds.

E.   Embezzlement

1. Definition
   Embezzlement is the fraudulent conversion of the property of another by one who is already in lawful possession.
   a. Fraudulent conversion
      i. Serious and substantial interference with the ownership rights of another.
      ii. Movement of property is not enough. The depriver must do something to assume ownership.
   b. Of another's property
      i. Real property; or
      ii. Personal property.
      iii. Not entitled to ownership rights at the time of the conversion.

   c. Already in lawful possession includes:
      i. Bank tellers stealing money;
      ii. Attorney stealing money from a client or the firm;
      iii. Truck driver selling the company truck;
      iv. Friend, who was given possession of a watch to hold, selling it to someone else.

2. Return Demand
   A demand of return is not necessary to sustain a conviction for embezzlement, but is evidentiary that embezzlement occurred.

3. Mens Rea
   An honest belief, even if unreasonable, that the defendant is the owner of such property is sufficient to acquit.

F. Receiving Stolen Property

1. Definition
   The crime of receiving stolen property is receiving stolen property, knowing it to be stolen, with the intent to deprive a superior owner of possession.

2. Elements

   a. Receiving
      i. Actual reception; or,
      ii. Constructive reception.

   b. Stolen Property.

NOTE: Once the item is back in the owner's hand or with law enforcement then it is no longer stolen. For example, Peter steals a guitar from Paul. Paul plans to make the sale to Mary but is caught by law enforcement. Mary knows the item is stolen but still wants to buy it. Paul tells all to the police and the police set up a sting. The police have Paul sell the guitar to Mary. After the sale, the police arrest Mary for receiving stolen property. Mary cannot be convicted because once the guitar went into the hands of the police it was no longer stolen.

---

   c. Knowingly
      The defendant must know or have reason to know that the object was stolen. The intent may be inferred by circumstantial evidence. For example, Billy Joel never had a dime in his life and Christy knew it. On Christy's birthday Billy Joel gave Christy a diamond necklace named "Uptown Girl". Christy has reason to know that the gift was stolen.

   d. Intent to deprive
      The defendant at the time of reception or thereafter must have intended to deprive a superior owner of the item.

2. Conviction

The thief cannot be convicted of receiving stolen property. However, another party to the crime who did not actually take the item (e.g., look-out man) can be convicted of receiving stolen property when they divide the stolen property.

IX.   ATTEMPT

A. Mens Rea

1. Definition.
    The defendant must have intended to do the crime for which he is charged for attempting.

2. Substantially Certain Test
    If a reasonable person knew or should have known that a consequence would result from their actions then it was enough for intent. *See also* MPC § 5.01.

3. Reckless or Negligence Crimes
    By nature there can be no attempt for these types of crimes because there is no intent.

4. Circumstantial Evidence
    The prosecution can use circumstantial evidence that the person had the intent.

B. More than Mere Preparation

1. Former Test
    "Last Act Test" - What was the last act and does it conform to attempt?
2. Proximity Test
    How close does the defendant come to completing the offense?

    a. Overt Act
        A person who does more than plan is guilty. For example, a person plans an arson and places combustible materials in the building to be used at a later date is guilty of attempted arson. *See Commonwealth v. Peaslee,,* 117 Mass 267 (1901).

    b. Some preparation in and of itself is not enough. Preparation must be done in furtherance of the crime itself. For example, defendant learned of a delivery by a person. The defendant went out in search of the person but could not find him to rob. Defendant's conviction for attempted robbery is reversed and a new trial ordered. *See People v. Rizzo* 246 N.Y. 334.

    c.   Probable Desistance Test

The defendant's actions must go so far that the defendant could not change his mind about the act. For example, a prisoner arranges to have tools delivered to his cell from the outside. In a routine search of incoming material, the prison officials discover the tools. The prisoner is not guilty of attempted escape because the prisoner had plenty of time to change his mind. *See Commonwealth v. Skipper*, 222 Pa. Super. 242, 294 A. 2d 780 (1972).

    d.   Reasonable Person Test

This test dictates that if a person goes beyond the point at which a reasonable person would stop the act, then it is an attempt.

    e.   Solicitation is not enough.

A person must go beyond soliciting for assistance. Solicitation may be a crime but it is not attempt. For example, a man wanted his mistress killed and asked an undercover police officer to do it. The man is not guilty of attempted murder. However, the same man who solicits murder and also provides the undercover police officer a gun to be used could be guilty of attempted murder.

3.   Equivocality Test

This test requires that the criminal unequivocally possess intent to commit the crime. Once the person decides to follow through with the crime, he is guilty of attempt if any step is taken to fulfill the crime. Under this approach, solicitation is enough.

4.   MPC § 5.01(1)(c)

    a.   Definition.

The MPC adopts the Substantial Certainty Test. The MPC defines an attempt as being satisfied when under the circumstances, the defendant believes he has acted in a way which constitutes a substantial step in a course of conduct planned to culminate in the defendant's commission of the crime.

b. **Elements.**
    i. Corroborating evidence is needed.
    ii. Close proximity is not necessary.
    iii. The following are examples of attempt in MPC:
        A) Lying in wait, searching for or stalking the victim (*contra People v. Rizzo, supra*);
        B) Enticing the victim to the scene of the crime;
        C) Reconnoitering the crime scene;
        D) Entering unlawfully;
        E) Possessing materials used or relating to the crime;
        F) Soliciting.

C. Impossibility of Crime

1. **Legal Impossibility**
This is where the action is not against the law and is never a crime. For example, Caitlin believes biting the state tree is a crime. In reality it is not. Caitlin states in protest of the government's taxing scheme she will break the law by biting a state tree and does so. Even though Caitlin had a guilty mind, there is no crime.

2. **Factual Impossibility**
Mistake of fact is almost never a defense to the charge. For example, A wants to murder B. B is already dead. A sneaks up behind B who is slumped in his chair and shoots him in the head. A is probably guilty of attempted murder.

D. Renunciation

1. **Definition**
The act of a person going forward with the crime (attempt) but then changes his mind and abandons the crime is considered a renunciation. The attempt element is already satisfied.

2. MPC

    MPC § 5.01(4) accepts renunciation (abandonment) as a defense. Under the MPC, though, the abandonment must be voluntary by the perpetrator. If someone coerces A not to go through with it, that is not voluntary. Sometimes a person (if with others) must attempt to stop the perpetration of the crime by the others even though he has already backed out of the plan.

X. ACCOMPLICE LIABILITY AND SOLICITATION

A. Criminal Parties

One may be guilty of asking another to break the law or of assisting another in breaking the law.

1. Principal in the First Degree
    This is the person who actually performs the crime (*actus reus*). Every crime that is perpetrated has at least one principal in the first degree. For example, the person who walks into the bank with the gun and holds it up is a principal.

2. Principal in the Second Degree
    This is a person who is present at the time of the crime, aids and abets in the commission, but does not participate in the crime (*actus reus*). For example, the look-out or driver at the bank robbery is a principal in the second degree.

3. Accessory Before the Fact
    This is the person who aids and abets the crime rather than committing the *actus reus* and is not present at the commission of the crime. For example, the person who supplied the guns or the vault plans to the bank.

4. Accessory After the Fact
    This is the person who did not participate in the planning or commission of the crime but furnishes assistance after-the-fact so that the perpetrator will not be caught. For example, after the robbery John goes over to his sister's house, admits robbing the bank, and asks if he can hide there. If she allows him, she is an accessory after the fact.

B. Procedural Issues on the Involvement of Person

1. Merger of Second-Degree and Before-the-Fact
   Most states have abolished the difference between Principal in the second degree and accessory before the fact. All participants are known as a principal.
2. Penalties
   All of the principals are subject to the same penalties. However, in practice, the non-committing principals usually receive a sanction that is less harsh than that of a principal in the first degree.

C. Accomplices

An accomplice is a person who aids, abets, encourages or assists another to perform a crime.

1. Words
   Words are sufficient to constitute a crime if the person's intent is to encourage criminal behavior.
2. Mere Presence not Sufficient
   Mere presence at the crime scene is not enough for criminal liability. The prosecution must show that the presence of the person was intended to encourage, aid, or abet the crime in some way.
3. Presence Plus Flight
   The presence of a person plus the fact that the person flees the scene of the crime is not enough to hold criminal liability. This is circumstantial evidence, but without something more it is not enough to convict.
4. Intervention
   a. Failure to Intervene
      Failure to intervene is not enough to constitute status of accomplice.
   b. Duty to Intervene
      Failure to intervene when there is a duty to intervene could lend itself to accomplice criminal liability. It would depend on the relationship and reasons why the duty-bound person failed to intervene.

5. Attempted Assistance Enough
    If a person attempts to encourage, aid or abet another and the perpetrator does not use such assistance the person is still held criminally liable under accomplice theory.
    See MPC § 2.06(a)(ii).

D. Mens Rea

1. Definition
    To satisfy the *mens rea* requirement, the person needs only to have intentionally aided or encouraged another's criminal act and intend for that other person to commit the crime.

2. Elements.

    a. Intentional Acts
        The accomplice must wish and intend for the other parties to commit the criminal act, plus commit an act (or omission) to aid toward the commission.

    b. Knowledge
        If the person knows the criminal wants to commit the crime and assists, the person is not guilty unless they knew they were assisting the criminal perform the criminal act.

For example, Dillinger says for three weeks he's going to rob the bank eventually. Dillinger then asks Al to borrow his car. Al lends his car. Dillinger uses the car to rob the bank. Al is not guilty as an accomplice unless the prosecution can prove that when Al lent Dillinger the car, he knew Dillinger was going to use it to rob the bank.

---

    c. Reckless Intent with an Automobile
        When an owner of a car lends his car to a person who he knows is drunk and the drunk gets into an accident, some courts hold accomplice criminal liability if the drunkenness is the proximate cause of the incident.

    d. Strict Liability
        If the crime is one of strict liability, most courts are unwilling to impose accomplice liability.

E. Accessory After the Fact

1. Definition.
   This is a person who knowingly gives assistance to a felon for the purpose of assisting the felon in avoiding apprehension.

2. Elements.
   The following are elements of accessory (not an accomplice):
   a. Completed felony;
   b. Knowledge of commission of a felony;
   c. Knowledge of the felon personally; and
   d. Affirmative acts to assist felon.

F. Solicitation

1. Definition.
   This crime occurs when a person requests or encourages another to perform a criminal act, regardless of the person's response. If the person agrees, then the crime is merged into conspiracy.

   For example, Eddie sees a transvestite walking down the road. Eddie pulls up in his Ferrari and offers money for sex. At that point, Eddie is guilty of solicitation.

2. Elements.

   a. No Act. No act is necessary. Words alone are sufficient.
   b. Attempt. Solicitation is equivalent to attempt in most states.

XI.   CONSPIRACY

A. In General

1.   Common Law

    a.   Definition
       Conspiracy is defined as an agreement between two or more people to do either an unlawful act or a lawful act by unlawful means.

    b.   Actus Reus
       Under traditional rules, the agreement was the overt act. Today, a majority of the states require an overt act in furtherance of the conspiracy. However, mere preparation will usually suffice if the preparation was done with the intent to complete the crime.

2.   Three Requirements for conspiracy

    a.   Agreement
       Conspiracy is an agreement between two or more parties.

    b.   Objective of Agreement
       The objective is to carry out a crime which is unlawful or which is lawful but carried out in an unlawful manner.

    c.   *Mens Rea*
       Intent on the part of the defendant is to enter into the agreement.

3.   Merger

    a.   General
       In some jurisdictions (including the MPC), if the conspirators were successful and completed their crime, the crime of conspiracy "merged" into the completed crime. The members of the conspiracy could thereafter only be convicted of the substantive crime, not also for conspiracy.

     b.   Modern View
         Under modern law, the conspirators can be convicted of both the criminal conspiracy as well as the substantive completed crime. However, most judges give concurrent sentences.

4.   Criminal Liability of Co-Conspirators

     a.   In General
         One conspirator may be liable for aiding and abetting the other conspirators as an accomplice if he meets the requisite complicity standards.

     b.   Exception
         Even if he does not meet the above, each conspirator may be criminally liable for all the crimes of the conspirators if two requirements are met:

         i.   The crimes were committed in furtherance of the objectives of the conspiracy; and

         ii.   The crimes were a "natural and probable consequence" of the conspiracy, i.e., the crimes were foreseeable.

5.   Difference from Attempt
     In attempt cases, the law mandates that there be a *substantial step* towards the commission of the crime. At common law for conspiracy, the agreement is normally sufficient to constitute the crime. Concerning conspiracy, the law intervenes at an earlier stage than the planning of the crime.

B. Agreement

The elements of an agreement are:

1.   Communication of Objective
     All that is required is that the parties communicate their intention to pursue a joint objective.

2.   Implied Proof Sufficient
     Agreement need not be express agreement. May be implied by concert of action that they will pursue the same common objective, one guy keeps "going with the flow."

3. Aiding and Abetting
   For example, if Clint aids and abets Sylvester & Arnold in the commission of the crime but never makes an agreement with them, courts are split as to whether Clint can be criminally liable for conspiracy. Note, however, that the MPC holds that a person does not become a co-conspirator by aiding and abetting the conspirators if he does not reach an agreement with the conspirators.

4. Bilateral Agreement
   a. Traditional View - Bilateral
      A defendant cannot be criminally liable for conspiracy unless both people agree to conspire. When an undercover officer makes an agreement with person to undertake a crime and the person is caught in the process, the common law defense would be that there was no agreement because the undercover officer did not really agree. The defense would be valid.

   b. Modern View - Unilateral
      An agreement does not have to be bilateral. A unilateral agreement to conspire is sufficient. In the example listed above, the person could be convicted.

C. Mens Rea

1. In General

   a. Specific Intent
      Conspiracy is a specific intent crime.
   b. There are two types of specific intent:
      i. Intent to agree; and
      ii. Intent to achieve the objective of the conspiracy.

2. Intent to Agree to Commit

   a. The conspirators must intend to agree.
   b. The intent to agree can be inferred from conduct.

3. Objective
   a. *Mens Rea* to Complete
      This means that the defendants have at least the *mens rea required for* the *crime.*

    b.   Intention
        But it also means that they must have the *intention* to
        bring about that result.

    c.   Example

If Larry and Dennis plan to set a building on fire and they *know* that there are people in the building and they are *virtually* certain that the people will be killed, but do not *intend* for them to die, they can be liable for murder under the extreme indifference (grossly reckless standard). However, they cannot be liable for conspiracy to commit murder because they did *not intend* for the people to die.

---

   4. No Conspiracy
      Negligence, recklessness or strict liability crimes can never include conspiracy charges because these crimes are not intentional.

   5. Corrupt Motive Doctrine

       a.   Ignorance is an Excuse
          An exception to the rule that ignorance of the law is no excuse.

       b.   Defense
          This allows one to raise the defense against conspiracy if the defendant did not know his object was a crime.

       c.   Proof to Convict
          A conviction for conspiracy is probative that the defendants acted with an "evil purpose."

       d.   *Malum Prohibitum* Crimes
          The doctrine has been limited to *malum prohibitum* crimes.

       e.   MPC View
          MPC and most states reject this doctrine.

6. Supplying of Goods and Services Used in the Crime

    a. Intent
        The supplier of goods and services must have intended to
        further the criminal purpose. Therefore, it is insufficient
        that he merely knew that his acts might tend to enable
        others to pursue criminal ends.

    b. This situation arises when a vendor supplies his goods to
        others with *knowledge* that the goods may be used to
        further criminal ends. The supplier in such case will not
        be shown to have joined the conspiracy based on this
        mere knowledge. Some of the factors that may implicate
        him in the conspiracy are:
        i.   The nature of his sales shows that he has in some way
              acquired a part in the illegal gain or venture. For
              example, Sandra sells Rehnquist machine guns. Part
              of the deal is that Sandra gets 10% of all sales that
              Rehnquist makes with street gangs.
        ii.   He is supplying controlled commodities (e.g.,
              automatic machine guns, drugs, C-4 explosive).
        iii. A large proportion of the original seller's sales goes
              to the conspiracy.
        iv.   The supplier's participation in illegal activity is more
              likely to be found where the illegal activity is known
              to the supplier to constitute a *serious crime,* than
              where the end use is a misdemeanor.

    c. Specific Intent
        The supplier's knowledge must be reasonably specific.
        For example, the supplier provides a machine gun to a
        drug dealer. He tells the supplier that he will be using it
        on the "Colombian deal or something." This is probably
        not specific enough to convict defendant.

D. Objective of the Conspiracy

1. Traditional View - Unlawfulness
    It is immaterial that an agreement be one to commit a crime in
    order to render it a criminal conspiracy. All that was
    necessary was that the object of the agreement be something
    unlawful or that the parties intend to accomplish something
    lawful by unlawful means.

2. Modern View - Agree to Commit
The modern trend, as well as the MPC, is to limit conspiracies only to agreements to commit crimes.

3. Overt Act Requirement

   a. Traditional View
   The conspiracy is completed as soon as an *agreement was* made.

   b. Modern Trend
   Conspiracy requires an overt act in furtherance of the crime. (Similar to attempt).

   c. MPC
   The MPC limits the overt act to *non-serious* crimes. For more serious crimes (felonies), the agreement is sufficient.

4. Pinkerton Rule
Each member of the conspiracy, by virtue of his *membership alone,* was liable for reasonably foreseeable crimes committed *in furtherance* of the conspiracy.

E. Termination

1. Abandonment by All Conspirators
Defense is somewhat misplaced because by definition, the conspiracy is complete once the agreement is made, regardless of their subsequent actions.

2. Withdrawal by a Conspirator

   a. Affirmative Act
   The defendant must make an affirmative act that lets the other conspirators know he is out.

   b. Traditional View
   Common law again does not allow the withdrawal to act as a defense against conspiracy because the act is complete once the agreement is made.

   c. Modern Trend
   MPC permits defense so long as:
      i. Voluntary Renunciation
      For example, if JohnJohn's mom told him he could not go through with the crime and he does not, JohnJohn did not voluntarily withdraw, i.e., of his own volition.

ii. Thwarting the Crime
     The defendant thwarted the efforts of the conspiracy.
     Usually this mandates that the person inform law
     enforcement officials of the conspiracy.   Then,
     regardless of whether the police acted on the
     information, the person is free and clear (modern
     trend).   Traditional view is if the police do not
     succeed in thwarting the conspiracy, the defendant
     may still be criminally liable.

XII. DEFENSES

A. Some Rarely Used Defenses to Crime

1. Infancy

   a. Traditional
      i. Age Seven and Below
         Any child under the age of seven years old is conclusively presumed as being unable to have criminal intent and cannot be convicted of a crime.
      ii. Ages Seven and Fourteen
         Any child between the ages of seven and fourteen is also presumed as being unable to have criminal intent. However, this presumption is rebuttable upon a showing that the defendant knew what he was doing and that he knew that it was wrong.
      iii. Ages Fourteen and Older
         There is no similar presumption.

   b. Modern Trend
      Many states have changed the age grouping but the presumptions remain the same.

   c. Age Determination
      The age of the child on commission of the crime -- not at the time of the trial -- controls since several years may have passed since the crime was committed and the trial.

2. Intoxication

   a. Involuntary Intoxication
      This is always a defense to a crime if it acted to render the defendant incapacitated under the relevant test of the state. That is, if the state's insanity defense standards are met.

      i.   Did not know the substance taken intoxicates.

          A) If one knows it intoxicates and willingly takes, but does not anticipate the strength of the effects, then involuntary intoxication cannot be used - it is voluntary intoxication.

          B) Again, must satisfy the standards of the state's insanity defense.

      ii. Substance taken under duress, force, or threat of force.

  b. Voluntary Intoxication

This defense will negate a conviction only when the crime charged is a specific intent crime and the intoxication caused the intent to be void.

      i.   Murder in the First Degree

EXAMPLE: First-degree murder is a specific intent crime requiring premeditation. If the person was so drunk he decided to go out and kill someone and does so the intoxication blinded the person's true intent. Then in this case it was not first-degree murder.

---

      ii. Not general Intent Crimes

The person cannot use this defense against general intent crimes such as rape.

  c. Affirmative Defense

      i.   <u>Voluntary Intoxication.</u> The defendant must plead intoxication as an affirmative defense and prove two elements:

          A) The defendant was intoxicated;

          B) The intoxication was the proximate cause of the action. <u>or</u>

      ii. <u>Involuntary Intoxication</u>. In the case of involuntary intoxication the person must prove that he:

          A) One did not reasonably know that the substance was intoxicating; or

          B) was forced to take the substance.

3.   Entrapment
        This is a rarely used or if used, successful defense.

   a.   Definition
        The person committed the crime because they were
        induced into committing a crime that they would have
        otherwise not committed except for the inducement of the
        law enforcement officer.

   b.   Limitation
        The defendant cannot deny the fact he committed the
        crime. The defense pled in the alternative. That is, *I did
        not do it but if I did I was entrapped.*

   c.   Traditional View (Current federal)
        The law enforcement officer must have created the intent
        in the mind of the defendant to commit the crime and the
        person must not be predisposed to committing such a
        crime.
        i.   Created Intent
              The officer must have thought of the crime and the
              plan to carry it out.
        ii.   Predisposition
              The defendant cannot be predisposed to the type of
              crime.

EXAMPLE: Noriego has been caught selling drugs every month for a
year. The police approach Noriego about selling their drugs and set
up the whole plan. Noriego absolutely refuses, but the officer prods
until Noriego agrees (even if he agrees just so the officer will "get off
his back"). Noriego is already predisposed to committing the offense,
and the defense will be unavailable.

---

   d.   Modern View (Some states)
        The modern view of entrapment is whether a reasonable
        person would commit the crime in light of the law
        enforcement activity. More liberal view than the
        traditional view but is still extremely difficult to be
        successful.
        i.   MPC § 2.13
        ii.   Rationale. The rationale for the change is to curb and
              discourage police misconduct in eliciting criminal

conduct among its citizenry including former criminals.

e. Application at Trial
It is better to use the entrapment defense in a bench trial rather than a jury trial. Juries tend to be more unsympathetic to those who admit doing the crime but who still want to blame someone else.

4. Consent
One cannot be convicted if the victim agreed to the allegedly criminal act. Consent can be expressed or implied from the circumstances.

a. Reasonableness
The standard is whether in light of all the facts a reasonable person would believe that the activity was consented to.

b. Example of Consent
In football, a defender tackles the quarterback extremely hard. The quarterback cannot claim assault and battery. The quarterback gave implied consent to being touched and hurt in the line of the game.

c. Beyond Consent
If the activity goes beyond the consent then it is a crime. Given the same football scenario above except the defender uses a stick to stop the quarterback from throwing the ball (he hits him in the head), criminal liability exists. The implied consent is reasonable touching, tackling, and some hitting, not beating with a stick.

d. Revocable
The consent can be revoked and from that point forward the activity must be ceased. In boxing, any punches thrown after revocation of consent are an assault and battery. However, if someone is invited on the land and while on the land is told to leave, the person must be given a chance to leave. Trespassing does not occur at the exact moment he is asked to leave, but after a reasonable time given to the disinvited guest to leave has elapsed.

B. Necessity – Choice of Evils

1. Generally

   a. Common law - Traditional
   The defense may be raised when defendant has been forced to commit a criminal act, not by coercion from another person, but by other impersonal events or circumstances. The basic nature of the defense is that defendant has chosen the lesser of two evils.

   b. MPC
   The MPC defense is called "justification." Under MPC § 3.02(1)(a) the harm or evil sought to be avoided is greater than that sought to be prevented by that law defining the offense changed.

      i. Unlike common law, the MPC allows the defense where the source of the emergency is coercion by another person rather than an event.
      ii. The harm prevented must be greater than, not equal to the harm committed. The actor must believe that he was making a choice of the lesser of two evils.
      iii. The test for determining whether the harm avoided was greater than the harm committed is objective and is determined by a jury.

2. Requirements

   a. Greater Harm not to Act
   The harm sought to be avoided is greater than the harm committed.

   b. No Alternative
   There is no reasonable third alternative that would also avoid the harm.

   c. Imminence and Causation
   The harm must be imminent and not a mere future occurrence. The defendant's negligence or recklessness cannot cause the situation by putting himself in a position where the emergency would arise. If the crime committed is one that is satisfied by a culpability of negligence or recklessness, and the situation was created negligently or recklessly, the defense of necessity cannot be used.

d. Nature of Harm
    The nature of harm sought to be avoided is not usually
    required to be serious bodily harm (as must usually be for
    duress), but rather can be non-serious bodily harm or even
    property damage.

3. Cases

Regina v. Dudley and Stevens, 14 Q.B.D. 273 (1884)

Facts: Defendants were stranded at sea without food. They killed and
ate one of the castaways and were later rescued. They would not have
survived had they not acted as they did. Defendants raised the defense
of necessity, but were convicted.

Holding: Causing the death of an innocent person is not justifiable at
common law as a necessity. Under the MPC if taking a life is the lesser
harm (e.g., to save many more lives), the defense of necessity may be
used.

State v. Warshow, 138 Vt. 22, 410 A. 2d 1000 (1979).

Facts: An environmentalist criminally trespassed on a nuclear power
plant to prevent it from going on-line. The defendant attempted to use
the defense of necessity.

Holding: The defense of necessity was not allowed because, in
licensing the plant, the legislature had already balanced the harm and
determined that the benefit of having the power plant outweighed the
evil of any harm it may cause.

C. Duress

1. Definition
    The defendant is said to have committed a crime under duress
    if he performed the crime because a threat (to the defendant or
    other reasonably accessible person) by a sufficiently strong
    third person overcame that defendant's will.

2. MPC

   a. Unable to Resist
      Under the MPC, this defense is available where the threat to the defendant was sufficiently great that a reasonable person in defendant's situation would have been unable to resist.

   b. Objective and Subjective Standards
      The MPC takes into account stark tangible factors such as height, weight, size, age, and the relationship between the defendant and the third person. It is a combination of a subjective and objective analysis.

3. Elements
   The following elements constitute duress.

   a. Threat
      The defendant is threatened by a third person.

   b. Fear
      Such threat produces a reasonable fear of death or serious bodily injury in defendant.

   c. Imminent Harm
      The fear is that he or another close person (child, girlfriend or wife) will suffer immediate or imminent harm.

   d. Bodily Harm
      Such harm will cause death or serious bodily harm.

4. Alternatives
   If a reasonable alternative exists, the defense of duress cannot be used.

5. Source of threat

   a. Common Law
      In common law, the source of threat must be another person. It cannot come from natural forces, which would then constitute a defense of necessity.

   b. MPC
      The MPC does not explicitly require that duress come from another person. However, duress must be unlawful, so the implication exists in the MPC.

6. Availability

a. Common law
In common law, the defense of duress is not available for homicide (i.e., the intentional killing of another).

b. MPC
Under the MPC, duress cannot be used to exculpate a defendant of homicide. However, some states allow duress to reduce the severity of the crime.

c. Felony murder
i. Duress can be used as a defense to felony murder in most states.
ii. Duress is usually asserted against the underlying crime. If successful, duress defeats the felony murder charge because there is no felony.

7. Imminence of Harm
a. Common law
Harm has to be immediate and imminent.
b. MPC § 2.09
The MPC does not require that the harm be imminent. It merely requires that the harm be such that a person of "reasonable firmness" would be unable to resist.

D. Self-Defense

1. Definition
One has a right do defend oneself against the use of unlawful force with reasonable counter force.

2. Requirements

a. Resist Unlawful Force
The defendant must have been resisting the present or imminent use of unlawful force.

b. Reasonable Force
The degree of force must not be more than is reasonably necessary to defend against the threatened harm.

c. Deadly Force
Deadly force is force that is intended or likely to result in death or serious bodily harm. The force used by the defendant may not be deadly unless the danger being resisted was also deadly force.

d. Aggressor
The defendant must not have been the aggressor unless:

    i.   The defendant is the aggressor but uses less than deadly force, and the protagonist responds with deadly force. Defendant would then be justified in defending himself with deadly force; or

    ii. The defendant withdrew after his initial aggression and the other party continued the attack, the defendant then loses his status as initial aggressor and can defend himself.

e. Retreat
In some states, the defendant must retreat so long as he can do so with complete safety. However, there is no duty to retreat under the following circumstances:

    i.   Dwelling
The attack takes place within defendant's dwelling or by the modern view his place of work.

    ii. Not the Aggressor
This exception is valid only if the defendant was not the aggressor or the assailant was not another resident of the dwelling.

    iii. Non-Deadly Force
No retreat is required before the use of non-deadly force in almost any jurisdiction. However, if non-deadly force does not work, retreat is necessary before resorting to deadly force.
See MPC § 3.04(2)(c).

3. Effect of mistake

a. MPC
If the defendant's mistaken belief as to the need for force is reckless to negligent, the claim of self-defense is not available if the crime charged is one which may be committed recklessly or negligently.

b. Common Law
So long as the belief is reasonable, defendant will be able to use self-defense.

    i.   Reasonable belief takes into account the defendant's subjective knowledge and experiences and weighs them objectively. That is, what would another reasonable person in defendant's position with defendant's experiences do?

  ii. Belief must be an honest belief. The courts will judge whether the belief was truly held by the person at the time of the action.

 c. Perfect vs. Imperfect Defense

  i. Perfect

Justifiable. The defendant honestly and reasonably believed that self-defense was needed to prevent imminent bodily harm. Justifiability leads to acquittal.

  ii. Imperfect

Defendant honestly but unreasonably believed that self-defense was needed to defend against a perceived bodily harm. Defendant can still be convicted, but the offense may be reduced to a lesser offense or a lower degree.

  iii. Self-Defense

People v. LaVoie, 155 Colo. 551 (1964).

Holding: The court held that one who reasonably fears for his safety may assert self-defense. There are three questions to ask:

1. Does the defendant *need* to protect himself against the use of unlawful force?
2. Does the defendant *honestly* believe he needed to protect himself against the use of unlawful force?
3. Does the defendant *reasonably* believe he needed to protect himself against the use of unlawful force?

State v. Leidholm, 334 N.W. 2d 811 (1983).

Holding: The court articulated that the defendant is justified in using self-defense when under the circumstances as perceived by him his acts appeared necessary to protect himself from imminent harm. Critical factor is not whether defendant's belief was correct, but whether it was reasonable. In this case the court permitted evidence relating to the subjective beliefs of the defendant.

There are three different standards of reasonableness:

1. Objective Reasonableness: Normal tort reasonableness. What would an ordinary prudent person believe is reasonable?
2. Objective/Subjective Reasonableness: Would another person with the defendant's same physical characteristics and same life experiences faced with similar circumstances act in the same manner?
3. Subjective Reasonableness: Take all of defendant's physical traits and mental traits and even psychological evaluations and put yourself in his shoes to determine if he acted reasonably.

E. Insanity

1. General
    A person who is determined to have been insane at the time of the crime, by whatever definition used, cannot be convicted.
    a. Incompetency to Stand Trial
        Incompetency is different from insanity. The person was not under a disability at the time of the crime. However, if subsequent to the crime, the defendant becomes mentally unstable insofar as cannot assist in his defense, then he is incompetent.

    b. Removal of the Disability
        Once the person becomes competent again, the trial may proceed.

2. Five Tests Used for Insanity

NOTE: The defense must give pre-trial notice within a time period governed by state law of use of the insanity defense.

---

    a. M'Naghten Rule (Test)
        i.   Traditional Test.
             M'Naghten is the traditional test for insanity.

        ii. Definition
             A person is adjudged insane under this test if when the crime was committed the person did not know the nature or quality of his act or he did not know that the act was wrong.
             A) The defendant did not know nature or quality of the act. The mental impairment caused the person not to comprehend that doing one thing

results in another action. For example, pulling a trigger causes the gun to shoot.

    B) The defendant did not know the act was wrong. The person was unable to know that the act was legally or morally wrong.

  iii. Criticism

This rule allows for a person who was impaired to be convicted. If the person knows that killing is wrong but is unable to control his actions he can still be convicted.

b. Durham ("Product") Test

A person is adjudged insane under the Durham test if the crime was a product of any mental impairment suffered at the time of the crime.

  i. Modern Rules.

The Durham test has a more liberal interpretation than the M'Naghten rule.

  ii. Criticism

The standard gives very little guidance to juries on what constitutes insanity under this test and as such has been rejected.

c. Irresistible Impulse Test

This is basically the M'Naghten test with an added section. That is, those who are unable to control their conduct, or who have lost the "power to choose" right from wrong, may use the M'Naghten rule of defense.

  i. Substantial inability to control. Failure to take medication and insane act would result in conviction. It must be so substantial that the person lacked volitional control.

  ii. Right and Wrong

If a person could not distinguish or choose between right and wrong, then acquittal may be appropriate.

d. MPC § 4.01

The MPC merges irresistible impulse test with the M'Naghten Rule.

i. Test

A person is adjudged insane if at the time of the act defendant suffered from a mental disease or defect and he lacked substantial capacity to either

A) Appreciate the wrongfulness or criminality of the act; or

B) Conform his actions to the law.

ii. Substantial Impairment

Substantial impairment of volition is required.

iii. Criticisms

A) It is impossible to measure a person's ability to control oneself.

B) John Hinckley was acquitted under this rule.

e. Federal Test

This was a response to John Hinckley's acquittal of the attempted assassination of President Ronald Reagan. Congress narrowed the insanity defense essentially to the M'Naghten test plus the requirement of a mental disease or defect.

i. Test

Defendant is adjudged insane if the act was a result of a severe mental defect or disease and the person was unable to appreciate the nature and quality or wrongfulness of the act.

ii. Repudiates Prong of MPC

Such actions do not include actions that they cannot conform to the law.

3.   Diminished Capacity

    a.   Specific Intent Crime
       This defense is much like insanity in that it states the person was incapable of forming the specific intent to commit a crime. For example, the required elements of first-degree murder are premeditation and specific intent to commit the crime. If a person was under the influence of drugs, they did not have the specific intent to commit the crime. However, that does not preclude conviction on a lower-degree crime (e.g., murder in the second degree).

    b.   General Intent
       Diminished capacity does not influence conviction on a general intent crime (e.g., rape).

    c.   Advance Notice
       The defense does not have to notify the prosecution prior to the trial of the intent to use the defense of diminished capacity unlike the insanity defense.

TABLE OF CASES

INDEX

We welcome your comments on this publication. Please write us at Staff@LawReviewPublishing.com.

If you are an excellent student, please inquire about our student editor positions. We can be reached at (800) 371-1271.